JESUS
OF
ISRAEL

JESUS

OF

ISRAEL

By

MARCHETTE CHUTE

ROBERT H. SOMMER
PUBLISHER
HARRINGTON PARK, NJ. 07640

ISBN 0-933062-26-5

Library of Congress Catalog Card Number: 61-8429

FOR MOTHER,
like the other one

AUTHOR'S NOTE

I once wrote a biography of William Shakespeare, called *Shakespeare of London,* which was based entirely on contemporary materials. The many things which were later said about Shakespeare were not included, and only the evidence of his own day was accepted.

This book is an attempt to do the same thing, much more briefly, in the case of Jesus of Nazareth. As far as I know this particular approach has never been tried before, any more than it was in the case of Shakespeare, and a new way of looking at things can sometimes be illuminating.

The translation of Josephus I have used is that of The Loeb Classical Library, published in America by the Harvard University Press. The translation of the Dead Sea Scrolls is from *The Dead Sea Scrolls* by Millar Burrows, published by the Viking Press. The translations of the "Book of Enoch" and "The Testaments of the Twelve Patriarchs" come from *The Apocrypha and Pseudepigrapha of the Old Testament in English,* edited by R. H. Charles and published by the Clarendon Press. I am grateful for permission to use this material.

M. C.

INTRODUCTION

Nearly everything that is known about the life of Jesus is contained in the four gospels, those of Matthew, Mark, Luke and John. It is possible to get supplementary evidence from other parts of the Bible, from Roman history, from archaeological evidence, from the Talmud, from Josephus and from other Jewish writings of the period, but the basic information must come from the four gospels.

The word "gospel" means "good news," and there is no attempt in any of the gospels to give an objective, unbiased account of the life of Jesus. The men who wrote the gospels were not trying to be impersonal historians. They were men who had good tidings, and each gave them in his own way.

In general, the gospels of Matthew, Mark and Luke bear a fairly close resemblance to each other. Mark's is the briefest, Luke's the most beautifully written, Matthew's the most elaborately shaped. They differ somewhat on facts and on chronology, but in all three the main outlines of the life of Jesus are about the same, and his teaching is the same also.

A great difference is apparent when any of these three

is compared with the Fourth Gospel, the gospel of John. There is not only a difference in times and places and events, although some of these are fundamental enough. There is also a basic difference in approach.

John was not especially interested in what Jesus did. He was much more deeply concerned with who Jesus was. The Fourth Gospel is based squarely on a single claim that Jesus made for himself, and his actions and teachings are identified so closely with this claim that they cannot be separated.

Because the Fourth Gospel is so unlike the other three, many people feel that it is not reliable. They feel that the writer was not an eyewitness to the events he described and that he forged evidence to suit his own purposes, by using the name of the disciple whom Jesus loved. A note at the end of the Fourth Gospel states that the book was written by this disciple, "and we know that his testimony is true." (*John* 21:24) This postscript is considered equally unreliable, and a great many of the books about Jesus that were written in the late nineteenth and early twentieth centuries omit the testimony of John.

This position is not easy to maintain, since the evidence within the Fourth Gospel itself indicates that the writer knew what he was talking about. He knew that the pool by the sheep market in Jerusalem had five porches and that the six water jars at the wedding in Cana were made of stone and held between twenty and thirty gallons apiece. He is very well informed about the geography of Palestine and shows a more accurate knowledge than

the other three gospels of contemporary living conditions.
For instance, the first three gospels give a date for the
arrest of Jesus which a knowledge of Jewish religious
customs shows to have been impossible. A different dating, the one given by John, is the only one that could
actually have occurred.

There is a much more fundamental reason, however,
for respecting the authority of the Fourth Gospel.

The impact which Jesus made upon his own century
was not that of a teacher of ethics, a good and wise man
who unfortunately happened to be crucified. The impact he made was that of someone who stirred up the
population to the danger point because he was able to
heal the sick and raise the dead, and he is remembered
in the Talmud as one who "practiced sorcery" and therefore led the people astray.

The acts of healing that the Talmud calls sorcery are
described in all four of the gospels, case by case and often
in the most exact detail. They cannot be explained away
by the argument that they could not have happened.
Something did happen, for the impact that Jesus made
upon his own generation is an historical fact.

This impact was intensified by the results of the crucifixion. The early Christian church, which was made up
of about a hundred and twenty people who had known
Jesus personally, was quite willing to base the whole of
its message on the fact that he had risen from the dead.
Unless all normal historical evidence is to be wholly

dismissed, it is clear that something happened in Judea in the first century that had never happened before.

All four gospels bear record to what Jesus did. Only the Fourth Gospel makes it clear how he could have done it. Since this is the basic problem that must be solved in any life of Jesus, John is therefore the basic authority, the only writer in whose light the ministry of Jesus can be understood.

The four gospels have been interpreted in various ways and over many centuries. My interpretation is merely that of a single individual and, of course, has no authority unless it seems to be inherently reasonable. In any case, it is no substitute for reading the four gospels themselves, since they are the primary source from which any understanding of Jesus must come.

Certain things must be remembered, however, in reading the gospels. The first is that they are being read in a translation, since the originals are in Greek. Luke was himself a Greek, which may account for the beauty with which he uses his native tongue; Matthew, Mark and John were not. But Greek was the great international language of the first century, known in every civilized country of the world, and it was therefore the quickest way to spread the "good news."

The translation which is most frequently used by English-speaking Protestants is the one made in England by order of King James at the beginning of the seventeenth century. It is the most familiar and the most beautiful of them all; but Biblical scholarship has advanced since then, and it has become clear that this version is not always accurate. For instance, Jesus said, "God is Spirit." (*John* 4:24) The translators of the seventeenth century mistakenly rendered this as "God is a spirit," which is quite a different thing.

Another disadvantage of the King James Version is that the language is not always as clear as it might have been. Luke wrote a very lucid Greek, but no one would guess it from the rather confused opening in the King James Version.

> Forasmuch as many have taken in hand to set forth in order a declaration of those things which are most surely believed among us, even as they delivered them unto us, which from the beginning were eyewitnesses, and ministers of the word; it seemed good to me also, having had perfect understanding of all things from the very first, to write unto thee in order, most excellent Theophilus, that thou mightest know the certainty of those things, wherein thou hast been instructed.

If the Greek sentence which Theophilus read were as blurred as that, it would have taken him some time to find out what Luke was really saying. But it was not, and in this case the Revised Standard Version gives a better translation.

> Inasmuch as many have undertaken to compile a narrative of the things which have been accomplished among us, just as they were delivered to us by those who from the beginning were eyewitnesses and ministers of the word, it seemed good to me also, having followed all things closely for some time past, to write an orderly

account for you, most excellent Theophilus, that you may know the truth concerning the things of which you have been informed.

Another modern translation, the one published by the University of Chicago, gives a slightly different impression of what Luke is saying.

Many writers have undertaken to compose accounts of the movement which has developed among us, just as the original eyewitnesses who became teachers of the message have handed it down to us. For that reason, Theophilus, and because I have investigated it all carefully from the beginning, I have determined to write a connected account of it for Your Excellency, so that you may be reliably informed about the things you have been taught.

The truth is that no single translation in English will convey precisely what the original writer intended to convey in Greek. Wherever there is a choice, each translator will naturally present what he himself thinks the writer may have meant; and since there have been nearly two thousand years of controversy on the subject of what the four gospels mean, it is not likely that there will ever be full agreement among translators. The writer of the present book has used the King James Version as far as possible, with an occasional alteration whenever it has been necessary.*

---

* I have changed into modern English some of the more archaic words in the King James Version, such as *wist* for *knew* and *noised* for *reported*. The Greek word *pneuma* is rendered in the King James Version as both *ghost* and *spirit,* since both words meant the same thing in the

There is another point to be remembered in reading the gospels. Some words can be accurately translated and still fail to convey the original meaning, because the point of view of the reader has changed. In the time of Jesus, for instance, the people who lived in Galilee believed that anyone who lived in Samaria was beneath contempt, and the phrase "a good Samaritan" would have been a contradiction in terms. That was why Jesus used the word in his parable, because he wanted to startle his listeners into understanding what he was saying. The point of the story is blunted and almost lost for a modern reader, because the phrase "a good Samaritan" now sounds quite natural.

There is another area of possible misunderstanding, and this is a much more serious one. The events in the four gospels took place nearly two thousand years ago, at a particular time in history and to a particular people. A great many mistakes have been made, and will continue to be made, as long as it is forgotten that these people were Jewish. Jesus was a Jew, his disciples were Jews, and so was nearly everyone else with whom he came into contact. In fact, the first great controversy that arose in the early Christian church was between those who felt that the "good news" Jesus brought was the exclusive

seventeenth century. This is no longer true, and I have retained the modern word for *pneuma*, which is *spirit*. I have restored the normal spelling of Old Testament names, some of which are altered in the New Testament, such as *Achaz* for *Ahaz* and *Elias* for *Elijah*. The seventeenth-century punctuation and the capitalization have been somewhat modified, and outright errors in translation have been corrected.

property of the Jewish people and those who felt it could be shared with the Gentiles.

Since then, the gospels and the rest of the New Testament have become the exclusive property of the Gentiles and it requires a deliberate act of historical imagination to remember that this was not always so. The background of the gospels is Jewish, and it is not possible to enter the world in which Jesus lived if that basic fact is ever forgotten.

JESUS
OF
ISRAEL

CHAPTER ONE

THERE was a race that had always loved God. As far back as the traditions of the Hebrews stretched, back into the dimmest tribal memories of the past, nothing mattered as much as their relationship to God. When they gave honor to their heroes, Abraham and Isaac and Jacob, they did not choose men who had been strong kings and mighty warriors. They chose men who had tried to come nearer to God and to be obedient to Him.

Usually they were called Jews, from a son of Jacob whose name was Judah, but their favorite name for themselves was Israel, which means "striver with God." This was a title of honor which had been bestowed on Jacob, and his descendants tried to be worthy of it.

When they arrived in Palestine as a small Semitic tribe, they found the local men of Canaan worshiping the fertility gods who would give them a good harvest. The newcomers themselves took up farming, and it was natural for them to be attracted to the religious practices of their neighbors. But they had brought with them, like a sword of steel, the words they never forgot: "Hear,

O Israel. The Lord our God is one Lord." (*Deuteronomy* 6:4)

Moses gave them that statement as he led them toward the land of Canaan, and he drove so deep into their hearts the conception of one God that it became indestructible. It survived exile and wars and persecution, and the more dangerous threats of relaxation and easy, beckoning religions. By the first century the Jews were still entrenched in Palestine, still convinced that they possessed a covenant with God and that they were His chosen people.

The other nations of the world looked upon them with a curious mixture of respect, exasperation and something approaching terror. It was rumored among the Greeks, for instance, that the Jews practiced ritual murder and offered victims from other nations as human sacrifices to their strange God. Anything alien and single-minded is always frightening, and in the practical, opportunistic world of the first century, with its many beliefs and its many gods, the Jews seemed very alien and very strange.

The Jews were not only the people of one God. They were also the people of one book, and the whole nation was reared in a knowledge of their holy Scripture. Every Jew knew of the faithfulness of Abraham and the greatness of Moses, the heroism of David and the works of Elijah, the splendor of Solomon and the bitterness of the Exile, the words of prophecy and the songs of praise— all the incomparable collection of writings that we now call the Old Testament. It was indeed a testament, a wit-

ness to the love of God that united a whole nation into
a single purpose.

The first five books of this Scripture of the Jews, the
books of Genesis, Exodus, Leviticus, Numbers and Deuteronomy, were believed to have been written by Moses;
and they contain a series of ordinances which made the
Jews the people not only of one God and of one book but
also of one Law. Some of these ordinances constituted a
moral and legal code, some of them were instructions for
the ritual of worship, and some of them were obviously
designed as health measures. But all of them were holy,
since the Jews believed that they were given to Moses as
the direct commands of God. A Jew named Josephus,
who was born about forty years after Jesus, said of them:
"It is an instinct with every Jew, from the day of his
birth, to regard them as the decrees of God, to abide by
them, and if need be, cheerfully to die for them."

Many Jews had died for them, counting death as nothing compared with disobedience to the law of the Lord.
When an alien conqueror tried to force the Jews from
their religion, seven brothers died under torture in a
single day, and their mother with them, because they
would not consent to eat the flesh of swine. "We are
ready to die, rather than to transgress the law of our
fathers."

Some of these laws grew very difficult to observe as the
Jews' manner of living changed with the centuries, and
some of them seemed trivial to outsiders. But all of them
were deeply important to the Jews, because they were the

outward and visible sign of the covenant that existed between God and His people. Every male Jew, for instance,
was required to wear a fringe on the border of his garment, not because the fringe mattered in itself but because it served as a reminder of one thing he must never
forget. "The Lord spake unto Moses, saying . . . 'It shall
be unto you for a fringe, that ye may look upon it, and
remember all the commandments of the Lord, and do
them.' " (*Numbers* 15:37, 39)

Under the law of Moses the Jews were bound together
by a series of difficult observances that reached down into
the smallest details of ordinary living; and they rejoiced
in them, for theirs was a willing service. As Josephus put
it, "Could God be more worthily honored than by such
a scheme, under which religion is the end and aim of the
training of the entire community? . . . Practices which
. . . other nations are unable to observe for but a few
days, we maintain with delight and unflinching deter-
mination all our lives." The difficult Law was not a bur-
den to the Jews. It was their special pride and their glory.

If the Law had existed by itself it might have destroyed
Israel, for it dealt chiefly with outward observances. But
side by side with it, and given almost equal honor, was
that other great legacy from the past, the words of the
prophets. The Law dealt with the letter of religion, but
the prophets dealt with its spirit. To the prophets of
Israel the love of God was a continuing, present reality,
and they taught the Jewish people how to fulfill the whole
of the law of Moses: "Hear, O Israel. The Lord our God

is one Lord: and thou shalt love the Lord thy God with all thine heart, and with all thy soul, and with all thy might." (*Deuteronomy* 6:4–5)

Through the prophets, the Jews had developed a sense of world mission. Because they had been faithful to God, salvation would come to all nations and vindication to the one nation that had served Him from the first. By the first century a dream had arisen—a dream so strong that it became an absolute conviction—that God would send a savior out of the line of David, who had been their greatest king, to rescue the Jews from their enemies and make the whole world realize the truth of their religion. This savior was given the title of Messiah, which means "anointed," because kings were anointed at their crowning as a sign of consecration. Sometimes, because so many Jews of the first century spoke Greek, he was called by the Greek word for anointed—*christos* or Christ.

Some of the Jews of the first century hoped and believed that the Messiah would be a political savior, and they had every reason for such a longing. The kingdom that had stretched so wide in the great days of Solomon had shrunk until it was little more than a marching ground for conquerors.

When Jesus was born, a king named Herod was on the throne of Judea. He was a remarkable ruler and did so much for the country that he was known as Herod the Great; yet he was merely what was called a client king, subservient to the power of Rome, and he obtained what privileges he could for the Jews through his own clever-

ness and his personal popularity with the Romans. Herod
was an Arab, and although he had been circumcised in
obedience to the Law and did his best to conciliate the
passionate people he ruled, the Jews never felt they could
trust him. Throughout his reign he was harried by political extremists, and Judea had many self-styled Messiahs
who hoped to bring about the kingdom of heaven by
force.

Nevertheless, this was a relatively small group, for the
power of the sword had never seemed as real to the Jews
as the power of the spirit. A much more characteristic
group looked for a different kind of Messiah, not a man
like other men but an almost supernatural being who
would act under the direct authority of God.

This view of the Messiah does not appear in the Old
Testament. It is the product of a later period, the one
that existed just before Jesus was born. Many Jewish
books were written during this period, and although they
were never accepted as Scripture some of them had a
profound influence.

One of the most influential of these Jewish works was
called the *Book of Enoch.* Parts of it had been in existence
for less than a hundred years, but the Jews of the first
century believed that it was very ancient. It bore the
name of the legendary Enoch, the great patriarch who
"walked with God," (*Genesis* 5:24) and it was supposed
to contain his visions of what would take place in the
age to come.

The *Book of Enoch* contains a very full description of

the Messiah. He is given the title of "the Son of Man" and
he is also called "the Elect One" and "My Son." He had
been appointed to his high office as the first act of God's
creation—"before the stars of heaven were made, his
name was named"—and "all who dwell on earth shall fall
down and worship before him." On the final Day of the
Lord he will sit on a throne of glory to judge the living
and the dead. All those who are worthy will receive "the
light of eternal life," for God and His son will abide with
them forever.

This description of the Messiah was believed in by a
great many Jews, including most of the followers of Jesus.
When Jesus said that he was the Messiah, the minds of his
followers naturally reverted to the prophecies in the
Book of Enoch and they waited confidently for the hosts
of promised angels and for the end of the world. When
nothing of the sort happened, the early Christian church
decided that Jesus would reappear on an imminent Day
of Judgment; and the three gospels of Matthew, Mark
and Luke contain descriptions of this Day, all echoing
the promise in the *Book of Enoch* that the Son of Man
would come with his angels to judge the living and the
dead.

This was not the Day of the Lord that the great prophets of the Old Testament had promised. They had not
taught that it would be either a political victory or a
supernatural cataclysm. To them, salvation would come
when Israel possessed a full understanding of God, and

the sign of its coming would be the end of all destruc-
tiveness.

> They shall not hurt or destroy
>   in all My holy mountain:
> For the earth shall be full of the knowledge of the Lord,
>   as the waters cover the sea.
>
> *(Isaiah* 11:9)

When Moses led his people toward the land of Canaan,
he set them on a path that involved something altogether
new in the history of the world; for Moses himself was
being pushed forward by his discovery of a new name for
God. This name was I AM. *(Exodus* 3:14) This was not
the title of some supernatural tribal ruler or even of a
kindly, protecting deity. This was reality itself.

For that reason, there was no spiritual decline after
Moses died, such as there usually is in a religion after
the death of its founder. The prophets of Israel who came
after him, men like Elijah and Isaiah, were not content
with preserving the discovery Moses had made. They set
out to discover for themselves the nature of this reality,
and each man gave in the name of God what he believed
to be the truth about Him. The great line of prophets
raised the conception of God and of man's relationship
to Him higher and higher, until it seemed impossible
that the time would fail to come when God would be fully
known.

In the end, when the savior did come, only the prophets themselves could have recognized him. He did not
come as a political conqueror or as the supernatural

judge of mankind. He described himself as "a man that hath told you the truth, which I have heard from God," (*John* 8:40) and the Day of the Lord he offered was the illumination of which the prophets had dreamed.

CHAPTER TWO

THE birth of Jesus is recorded in two gospels, those of Matthew and Luke. The two accounts disagree with each other at so many points that it is difficult to find out what really happened, and yet the problem is one that cannot be ignored.

Jesus was born to a woman named Mary at a time when the mood of expectation over the coming Messiah was at its highest. The waiting people did not all agree about the exact nature of the Christ who was to come, but nearly all of them were convinced that he would be born of the line of David. David had been their greatest king, faithful to God and triumphant over Israel's enemies; and three of Israel's greatest prophets, Isaiah, Jeremiah and Ezekiel, had all proclaimed that a savior would come of his line. The triumph of the coming Messiah was called "the reign of the house of David," and the Jewish nation waited in expectation for the Christ to be born of David's line. "Hath not the scripture said, that Christ cometh of the seed of David?" (*John* 7:42)

Matthew and Luke both realize that this point is of crucial importance and devote a great deal of space to

establishing it. The genealogies they present to the reader
are not quite the same, since Matthew traces the descent
through the tenth son of David, King Solomon, while
Luke traces it through an earlier son named Nathan. In
any case, the same point is established. Joseph, the hus-
band of Mary, is the direct descendant of King David.
It is therefore a fulfillment of prophecy that through his
line the Christ should come.

The angel who comes to Mary with the news that she
will bear a son reinforces this same point of a descent
through King David.

> He shall be great,
>   And shall be called the son of the Highest:
> And the Lord God shall give unto him
>   the throne of his father David.
>
> *(Luke* 1:32)

If Matthew and Luke had been free to leave the matter
there, they would have been fortunate, since the question
of Davidic descent was vital to their argument that Jesus
was the Messiah. Against this, however, they possessed
two very inconvenient pieces of information. The first
is a statement, made by Jesus himself and reported by
both Matthew and Luke, that the Christ was not the
descendant of King David. (*Matthew* 22:43–45; *Luke*
20:41–44) The other is a much more destructive piece of
evidence, one that makes the genealogical tables worth-
less.

The genealogical tables are based on Joseph; and both
Matthew and Luke report that Jesus was born of a virgin.

By including this piece of information, Matthew and Luke destroy the strongest argument they possessed that Jesus was the Messiah, since he could not claim descent from King David unless Joseph were his father. Moreover, the story is not only contrary to all human experience but is alien to Jewish training and culture. The Jews, with their respect for fatherhood, would be the last people on earth to evolve the idea of a virgin birth in connection with their coming Messiah. It is true that Matthew tries to get scriptural authority for the story by quoting a line from the prophet Isaiah: "Behold, a virgin shall conceive and bear a son." (*Isaiah* 7:14) But this is a slender reed to lean on, since the Hebrew word which Isaiah uses can equally well be translated "young woman" and since Isaiah also makes it clear that the child will be born in his own lifetime.

Matthew and Luke had every reason to omit a story which was not only unrelated to the idea of a Messiah but which in fact contradicted it. Since they did not omit it, the probability is that they could not. It must have come to them backed by an authority so unshakable that it could not be ignored, and the only human being who could have exerted this kind of authority was Mary herself. If she said that the child was born of "the holy spirit," (*Matthew* 1:18; *Luke* 1:35) and not of any physical law, they had no choice but to believe her.

The strongest single reason they had for believing Mary is to be found in the career of her son. Throughout the whole of his ministry, Jesus acted in direct contradiction to physical law, not once but over and over again, and all four gospels bear witness to that fact. They also bear witness to the fact that Jesus considered the fatherhood of God to be the rock on which he based his teachings. He once gave a direct commandment to his followers: "Call no man your father upon the earth; for one is your Father, which is in heaven." (*Matthew* 23:9) Jesus was convinced that the fatherhood of God was not an abstraction but a provable fact. This conviction was held by Mary also, so overwhelmingly that it was possible for her to bear a child without a human father.

Luke makes it clear that Mary was a devout Jewess, obedient to the Law in every particular. Nevertheless, as the result of what she clearly considered to be a direct message from God, she surmounted one of the most absolute of laws, the law that governs birth. "With God nothing shall be impossible." (*Luke* 1:37) In this, Mary belongs in the direct line of Israel's prophetic tradition, and the prophet she most resembles is Elijah.

The story is told of Elijah that he was living in the house of a widow when her son died. According to physical law, death is irrevocable. Nevertheless, Elijah took the dead child out of his mother's arms, carried him upstairs to the prophet's own room and laid him upon the bed. Then he demanded of God, "O Lord my God, hast Thou also brought evil upon this woman with whom I sojourn, by slaying her son?" (*I Kings* 17:20) Elijah apparently questioned that the child had died by the will of God, and it was this doubt which made him refuse to be-

lieve that the child's death was irrevocable. "And the
Lord heard the voice of Elijah; and the soul of the child
came into him again, and he revived." (*I Kings* 17:22)
Elijah brought the child downstairs again and said to his
mother, "See, thy son liveth." (*I Kings* 17:23)

It was an expectation among the Jews that Elijah
would be the forerunner of the Christ. "Behold, I will
send you Elijah the prophet before the coming of the
. . . day of the Lord." (*Malachi* 4:5) This was believed
to mean the physical presence of the prophet, but instead
it was his point of view that reappeared in Israel. Elijah's
conviction that nothing was impossible to God was shared
by Mary of Nazareth, and it was this conviction that was
the forerunner of the Christ.

The account of the virgin birth that is given in the
Gospel of Matthew is so brief as to seem almost reluctant.
It is given about half the space that Matthew gives to his
genealogical list of Joseph's ancestors. Luke, on the other
hand, tells the story at great length, and some of the details he gives are so precise that they would normally have
come from an eyewitness.

Luke wrote a sequel to his life of Jesus which is called
The Acts of the Apostles, and in it he states that Mary,
the mother of Jesus, was present in the upstairs room in
Jerusalem when the early church was formed. (*Acts* 1:14)
Luke also says of himself, at the beginning of his own
gospel, that he had done his research with great care. A
literal translation of the passage says that he "investigated
from their source all things accurately." (*Luke* 1:3) The

most obvious source for information about the birth of
Jesus was Mary herself. Luke would certainly have con-
sulted her if he could, and there was apparently nothing
to prevent him from having done so.

If Luke was in direct contact with Mary of Nazareth,
this would supply an explanation for the very feminine
quality of his narrative, which becomes all the more
noticeable when his version is compared with Matthew's.
Luke tells the story of the birth of Jesus from a woman's
point of view, while Matthew concerns himself with the
kind of information that a man would consider important.

Throughout the Gospel of Matthew, Mary is kept in
the background and Joseph is the chief actor in the
drama. It is Joseph, not Mary, who receives the message
from the angel, and in fact Joseph is visited three times
by an angel of the Lord. In each case Joseph obeys the
message and he initiates the action throughout, even to
the point of being the one who names the child Jesus.

The Gospel of Matthew also places a special emphasis
on the political background. Herod the Great takes a direct part in the action, behaving in a fashion that might
be expected of that dying and half-demented king, his
natural cruelty intensified by a long and agonizing disease. The political climate under his son Archelaus is
also described, and in general, throughout this whole
section, the details are those that would have interested
a male Jew. Even the genealogical table assigned to
Joseph is the one he would have preferred, with a glit-

ter of royal ancestors like Solomon, Ahaz, Hezekiah and Manasseh.

The genealogy that is given in the Gospel of Luke is quite different. It contains more names, and most of them are those of ordinary people. In fact, there is a very strong emphasis in Luke's version on humility, rising to its most beautiful expression in the song of Mary that is called the Magnificat.

> My soul doth magnify the Lord,
> And my spirit hath rejoiced in God my Saviour.
> For He hath regarded the low estate of His handmaiden:
> For, behold, from henceforth all generations shall call
>   me blessed. . . .
> He hath put down the mighty from their seats,
> And exalted them of low degree.
>
> (*Luke* 1:46–48, 52)

It is not with "the mighty" that the story in Luke is concerned, and there is no mention either of Herod the Great or of his son. Nor is there any mention of the three wise men of Matthew's gospel, who come to the newborn child with costly gifts of gold and frankincense and myrrh. In Luke's gospel, it is shepherds who come instead; and they find the baby not in what Matthew calls a house, but in a manger.

Even when Luke's information may be inaccurate, it is the kind of inaccuracy that would be natural for a woman like Mary. The Gospel of Luke states that Joseph and Mary lived in Galilee but came south to Judea because a census had been ordered by the Romans for tax purposes "when Cyrenius was governor of Syria." (*Luke* 2:2) Luke was aware of a census that had been conducted under this particular governor because he mentions it elsewhere (*Acts* 5:37), but this census took place in 6 A.D. It was held because the Romans had just deposed Archelaus as king of Judea and turned the country into a Roman province. It has been argued that the Romans conducted an earlier census also in Judea, but this is very unlikely. As long as Herod the Great was still alive, Judea did not pay tribute to Rome.

Luke's gospel goes on to say that when Joseph arrived in Judea he went "unto the city of David, which is called Bethlehem; because he was of the house and lineage of David." (*Luke* 2:4) It is conceivable that it was some local matter in connection with the holding of property that brought Joseph back to the town of his ancestors. Women of that period had very little connection with business matters, and Mary may not have had a clear recollection of the reason she and Joseph had gone to the crowded town of Bethlehem, where there was no room for them at the inn.

This was not Mary's first visit to Judea. A short time earlier she had been there for a three months' visit and had stayed in the hill country with a kinswoman of hers whose name was Elizabeth. Details as precise as this can only have come, directly or indirectly, from Mary herself, and Luke emphasizes that she forgot nothing. "Mary kept all these things, and pondered them in her heart." (*Luke* 2:19) The beautiful literary form in which the story is cast is certainly Luke's own contribution, but it is difficult to see how the details could have come from anyone but Mary.

The child who was born in Bethlehem was named Jesus. The meaning of the word in Hebrew is *savior,* and that may be the reason he was given the name. On the other hand, it was a very common name among the Jews, as common as Mary or Joseph.

Eight days after his birth, Jesus was circumcised. (*Luke* 2:21) This was the ceremony that set the Jews apart from all other nations in their own eyes, the act that the Lord had demanded of Abraham. "He that is eight days old shall be circumcised among you, every man child in your generations . . . And the uncircumcised man child whose flesh of his foreskin is not circumcised, that soul shall be cut off from his people; he hath broken My covenant." (*Genesis* 17:12, 14) Already the eight-day-old child was set apart from the children of all other nations, marked with the outward sign of his people's covenant with God.

For over a month after the birth of her child, Mary continued with what Luke calls "the days of her purification according to the law of Moses," (*Luke* 2:22) the thirty-three days that were demanded by the Jewish law. Then she and Joseph left Bethlehem and journeyed six miles with the child to Jerusalem, "to present him to the Lord . . . and to offer a sacrifice." (*Luke* 2:22, 24)

The Jews had no local altars or places of worship as other religions had; all their acts of sacrifice and devotion took place at the great Temple in Jerusalem. As

Josephus put it, "We have but one temple for the one God . . . common to all as God is common to all." Every Jew in the world paid his half shekel to the Temple fund, and those who were too far away to make a direct payment set up banks in the major foreign cities. "They made use of these cities as a treasury, whence, at the proper time, they were transmitted to Jerusalem."

When Herod the Great became king, he rebuilt the Temple into a glory of marble and gold, keeping the original dimensions but using all the architectural knowledge that had been developed since. It took over eighty years before the elaborate structure was completed, but when Mary brought her son to the Temple it was already one of the show places of the ancient world.

At the base of the splendor and the gold lay the rock on the hill that had once been a threshing floor. David made it into an altar to the Lord and it became the Holy of Holies. In any other religion this sacred area would have housed the image of the god, but the God of the Jews had no image.

When the time of her purification had ended, Mary brought Jesus to the Temple and offered the sacrifice that was demanded by the Law. This was a young lamb if she could afford it, and if not "two turtledoves, or two young pigeons." (*Leviticus* 12:8) Evidently Mary was not rich enough to offer a lamb since she made a gift of birds. "And when they had performed all things according to the law of the Lord, they returned into Galilee, to their own city Nazareth." (*Luke* 2:39)

Matthew contradicts this story of Luke's and gives an entirely different account of what happened after Jesus was born, supporting it by a series of quotations from Scripture. According to Matthew, Joseph took Mary and Jesus into Egypt, to escape the wrath of Herod and to fulfill the words of the prophet Hosea, "Out of Egypt have I called My son." (*Matthew* 2:15) After that, "he came and dwelt in a city called Nazareth; that it might be fulfilled which was spoken by the prophets, he shall be called a Nazarene." (*Matthew* 2:23) Matthew had already stated that Jesus had been born in Bethlehem to fulfill a prophecy uttered by Micah and that Herod's massacre of the innocents had been foretold by Jeremiah.

The story that Matthew tells is much more complicated than the one in the Gospel of Luke, which is simply the story of a Jewish girl making an offering in Jerusalem and going back to her home in Nazareth. Luke's version seems more probable, especially since Matthew is a little inconsistent. Matthew says that Joseph went first to Egypt and then to Nazareth in Galilee because he was "afraid" to go back to Judea (*Matthew* 2:22) as long as Herod the Great or his son Archelaus was ruling there. Archelaus was deposed in 6 A.D. and Joseph could have returned with his family then. But he did not, and therefore Luke's account would seem to be the correct one: Joseph lived in Galilee, not in Judea, and when he went to Nazareth he was returning to his "own city." (*Luke* 2:39)

The gospels agree that Jesus was brought up in Galilee,

and Matthew himself gives a little sketch of the local
reaction in Nazareth to his ministry. "Whence hath this
man this wisdom, and these mighty works? Is not this
the carpenter's son? Is not his mother called Mary? And
his brethren, James, and Joses, and Simon, and Judas?
And his sisters, are they not all with us? Whence then
hath this man all these things?" (*Matthew* 13:54–56)

Every year, in the spring, the family left Nazareth and
made the seventy-mile journey south to Jerusalem. They
went "every year at the feast of the passover," (*Luke* 2:41)
the great festival of rejoicing when the Jews came to the
Temple from all over the civilized world to commemorate
the time when their ancestors were released from bondage in Egypt. "The Lord thy God brought thee forth out
of Egypt by night. Thou shalt therefore sacrifice the passover unto the Lord thy God . . . in the place which the
Lord shall choose to place His name there." (*Deuteronomy* 16:1–2)

When Jesus was twelve years old the family went to
Jerusalem as usual and when the seven days of the festival
were ended turned homeward to Galilee. "The child
Jesus tarried behind in Jerusalem, and Joseph and his
mother knew not of it. But they, supposing him to have
been in the company, went a day's journey; and they
sought him among their kinsfolk and acquaintance. And
when they found him not, they turned back again to
Jerusalem, seeking him. And it came to pass, that after
three days they found him in the temple, sitting in the

midst of the doctors, both hearing them, and asking them questions. And all that heard him were astonished at his understanding." (*Luke* 2:43–47)

Mary had been very frightened, but the reproof she gave Jesus was a gentle one. "Son, why hast thou thus dealt with us? Behold, thy father and I have sought thee sorrowing." (*Luke* 2:48) It was of course Joseph to whom Mary was referring, but Jesus would not agree to that use of words. "How is it that ye sought me? Did ye not know that I must be about my Father's business?" (*Luke* 2:49)

During the course of his ministry Jesus consistently refused to call Mary his mother; and at the crucifixion, when he gave her into the care of the disciple he loved the most, his words to her were, "Woman, behold thy son," and to John, his disciple, "Behold thy mother." (*John* 19:26, 27) Jesus refused to use either "father" or "mother" in the sense of an originator of life, and the fatherhood of God which the Jews spoke of figuratively was to Jesus a literal fact.

It is clear that Mary had known the same conviction, however momentary it may have been in her case. Luke uses the terminology of his own day and describes this illumination as an angel of the Lord coming to her, but the nature of the conviction itself is very clear.

> The holy spirit shall come upon thee,
> And the power of the Highest shall overshadow thee;
> Therefore also the holy thing which shall be born of thee
> Shall be called the son of God.
>
> (*Luke* 1:35)

When Mary spoke to her twelve-year-old son in Jerusalem and called Joseph his father, she was speaking as the world speaks. Jesus did not use words in that fashion. They returned to Galilee, and again Luke emphasizes that Mary did not forget what had happened. "His mother kept all these sayings in her heart." (*Luke* 2:51)

CHAPTER THREE

GALILEE was a small pocket of land, about fifty miles long and twenty-two wide, which lay to the north of Judea and Samaria. It was ruled over by Herod Antipas, who was one of the many sons of Herod the Great. When his brother Archelaus of Judea was deposed by the Romans, he became the senior member of the family and the gospels call him Herod or King Herod. He was no worthy son of Herod the Great, and one of his subjects, Jesus of Nazareth, called him "that fox." (*Luke* 13:32)

King Herod ruled a beautiful land. Nearly the whole kingdom was under cultivation and Josephus describes it as "one great garden." Galilee was famous for its wheat and rich in grapes and olives, while all sorts of fruits and vegetables could be grown so easily that the peasants lived comfortably on their small holdings.

The Jewish farmers of Galilee cultivated the land well, with their wives and children helping them. They did their plowing and sowing in the autumn when the first rains had loosened the soil. The barley was reaped in the early spring, and on the second day of Passover a sheaf of barley was offered as the first fruits of the coming harvest. The wheat was reaped a little later, in May or June, and the heavy crop of fruit was gathered in September.

The Jews of Galilee were an agricultural people, still moving to the ancient rhythms of seedtime and harvest that Jesus used as the basis of so many of his parables. To a certain extent this was true of all the Jews in Palestine. The Law made no provision for finance or commerce, and a good Jew like Josephus could speak rather condescendingly of the "mercenary devotion to trade and commerce" that characterized the people along the seacoast. Half the Jews in the world lived outside Palestine and had adjusted themselves quickly to the life of the big cities. A Jewish banking house had developed very early in a city on the Euphrates, and since then the Jews had prospered in many parts of the world. They were still faithful sons of Israel and obedient to the Law, but they lived a different life from the Jews of Palestine, who were mostly farmers as their ancestors had been. When they used a business term it was likely to be Greek, for Greek was the great international language of trade and the one used by businessmen everywhere.

In Galilee the large cities were also Greek, with forums and stadiums and the images that the Jews considered blasphemous. Greek urban civilization, with its strength and its attractiveness, was as evident in Galilee as it was everywhere else in that part of the world. But the smaller towns and villages were still Jewish, still clinging to the ways of their forefathers and refusing to be carried along by the tides of new civilizations as their ancestors had refused so many times before.

The Galileans were a difficult people to rule. Herod was a tetrarch, a minor princeling who held his throne only so long as he stood in the good graces of the emperor, and he and his subjects were expected to pay tribute to Rome. When the Romans conducted their tax census in 6 A.D., Judas the Galilean bitterly reproached his fellow Jews for "recognizing the Romans as masters when they already had God." Galilee was still full of such men, waging an unceasing guerilla warfare against their overlords and refusing to honor king or emperor because honor must be given to God alone. Josephus said proudly of the men of Galilee that they were "from infancy inured to war. . . Never did the men lack courage or the country men." King Herod found them difficult to control, and there was a constant ferment, both political and religious, just below the surface of that lovely and apparently peaceful land.

One of the most beautiful parts of Galilee was the section in the southwest around Nazareth. The town itself, as Luke says, was on a hill, one of the gentle hills of Lower Galilee that are so unlike the fiercer hills of Judea. Cut off from the sea and from the main trade routes, the town lay cradled in the ancient rhythms that the Jewish peasants had managed to maintain in spite of all the strange winds and foreign civilizations that surrounded them. The cities of Galilee might be Greek, but the country towns like Nazareth were wholly Jewish.

Within the family itself, it was the mother who maintained from generation to generation the continuity of domestic ritual that surrounded a Jewish child as soon as it was born. The Law held her in high esteem, and the fifth commandment of Moses gave her an equal position with the head of the household, the father himself. "Honor thy father and thy mother, as the Lord thy God hath commanded thee." (*Deuteronomy* 5:16) If a Jew treated either of his parents with contempt, or if, as Josephus puts it, there was "the slightest failure in his duty towards them," the legal punishment was death. Jewish criminal law was on the whole merciful, but this was one crime that could not be condoned.

> My son, keep thy father's commandment,
> And forsake not the law of thy mother . . .
> When thou goest, it shall lead thee;
> When thou sleepest, it shall keep thee;
> And when thou awakest, it shall talk with thee.
> (*Proverbs* 6:20, 22)

The children of the household took part from the first in the ceremonies and the teachings that bound the members of the family so closely together and bound them all to God.

One of the most beautiful of the ritualistic acts had only lately been introduced into Jewish households. This was the lighting of the lamp at the beginning of the Sabbath by the mother, and only if there was no woman in the household could a man light the Sabbath lamp. The prayer that was ultimately used in connection with the ceremony was based on the beautiful passage from the Psalms: "In Thy light shall we see light." (*Psalms* 36:9)

The Sabbath began at sundown, for the Jews followed the reckoning that is given in Genesis: "And the evening and the morning were the first day." (*Genesis* 1:5) The Sabbath fell on the seventh day of the week, and again the Jews were following the rhythm that was recorded for the creation. "On the seventh day God ended His work which He had made; and He rested on the seventh day from all His work which He had made. And God blessed the seventh day, and sanctified it." (*Genesis* 2:2–3) Later on, the Christians changed their Sabbath to the first day of the week, which is Sunday, but for the Jews it was the seventh day that remained holy.

Since their whole way of life was based on the word of God, and since it was a written word, the education of their children was deeply important to the Jews. As Josephus said, "We pride ourselves on the education of our children." The Jews honored learning and made it available to anyone who was able to receive it; and a boy like Jesus, brought up as the son of a carpenter, learned to read and to know his Scripture well.

The purpose of learning was to study the Law, and the chief place it was studied was the synagogue. Each Jewish village had its synagogue, and the great city of Jerusalem had nearly five hundred. It was the creation of the people themselves and the cornerstone of the life of the community. Every Sabbath in Nazareth, the villagers gathered together with one of their number chosen as leader, to listen to the Law being read aloud and to comment upon it.

The synagogue probably originated during the days of the Babylonian Exile, when the people were scattered, the Temple lay in ruins and only the Scripture remained. By now there were Jewish synagogues all over the world, for they could come into existence wherever ten men were gathered together and could be conducted in any language. The Scripture was read aloud in Hebrew and then translated immediately into the vernacular. This had been done ever since the days of Nehemiah, so that the people could "understand the reading." (*Nehemiah* 8:8)

In Galilee the vernacular was Aramaic, which was the spoken language of all Palestine. Very few Jews of the first century understood Hebrew, any more than the average Christian of today understands Latin, and it remained a holy language in which the Scripture was safely embedded until it could be brought out and discussed on the Sabbath.

Like everyone else, Jesus spoke Aramaic. A few of his statements in that language have survived directly in the gospels, the *Talitha cumi* with which he told a dead child to rise, (*Mark* 5:41) and the *Ephphatha* with which he freed a man who was deaf and dumb. (*Mark* 7:34) He once quoted from Scripture in Aramaic, although Luke makes it clear that Jesus was able to read Hebrew.

It took a long time to read the whole of the Law in the

synagogue, since only one verse from Moses could be read
at a time, or three verses from the prophets. After the
selection from Scripture had been read aloud to the as-
sembled people, the passage was commented upon by a
rabbi, an expounder of the Law. This was not a formal
office, and any man was welcomed into the synagogue if
he were sufficiently learned to be a teacher. Jesus was
called a rabbi by the people of Galilee, and he did most
of his teaching in the synagogues.

When Josephus was describing the function of the
synagogues, he remarked that the Law "left nothing,
however insignificant, to the discretion and caprice of the
individual." This was true in one sense; all Jews did the
same thing at the same time in the same way. But this
similarity of observances did not extend to any similarity
of creed, and from the great root of the Jewish faith in
one God there had grown a variety of theories and opin-
ions.

One Jewish sect, the Sadducees, did not believe in the
resurrection of the dead or in a future system of rewards
and punishments. Another sect, the Pharisees, took a re-
verse position and believed in a future life and a day of
judgment. They also held to an unusually high standard
of personal conduct. An even more devout group were the
Essenes, who gave up all ownership of property, dressed
only in white and lived in rigidly controlled communi-
ties. Josephus says that in their clothes and behavior the
Essenes resembled "children under rigorous discipline,"
and so in a way they were, good children who withdrew

from the world to prepare themselves for a life to come. There were also men who knew no community and lived by themselves in the wilderness. In his youth Josephus stayed for a time with one such hermit, and he followed each of the sects in turn; but in the end he reached the conclusion that the Pharisees had the wisest and best way of life.

The Pharisees were the most influential of all Jewish sects, for they were the party of the people. The Sadducees were mostly conservative aristocrats, with little to offer the ardent dreams of the Jews, and the Essenes held aloof from normal living. It was the Pharisees who interpreted the Law so that ordinary people could follow it, doing most of their teaching in the synagogues, and it was the Pharisees who converted many Gentiles to Judaism. Working with them were the scribes, who were responsible for the accurate copying of the Law, and together they had a profound influence on the community. It was chiefly the Pharisees with whom Jesus came into contact, and some of them became his followers.

Like any other religious group, the Pharisees had their weaknesses. Some of them were ostentatious in their religious zeal, some were hypocrites and some overvalued the recognition of the world. But in general they held to a higher ethical standard than any group except the Essenes, without that withdrawal from the world which made it so much easier for the Essenes to be virtuous.

A great many of the teachings of Jesus that are recorded in the gospels were not original with him. It was the Pharisees who first gave them expression. One of the greatest of the Pharisees was a rabbi named Hillel who lived in the days of Herod the Great and who taught what Christians call the Golden Rule. "Do not unto others as you would not that they should do unto you." A book was written by a Pharisee a few generations before the birth of Jesus and called *The Testaments of the Twelve Patriarchs;* and in it there is taught what has been called a Christian view of forgiveness. "These things, therefore, I say unto you . . . my children, that ye may drive forth hatred, which is of the devil, and cleave to the love of God. . . . Love ye one another from the heart; and if a man sin against thee, speak peaceably to him . . . and if he repent and confess, forgive him. . . . And if he be shameless and persist in his wrong-doing, even so forgive him from the heart."

Jesus has sometimes been represented as being merely a teacher of morality, but if he had been that and nothing more there would have been no reason for the Pharisees to have feared him. A great many of his teachings as they are recorded in the Gospel of Matthew are merely an expression of the highest Jewish morality of the period, strange to the Gentiles who later became converted to Christianity but perfectly familiar to anyone who knew the teachings of the Pharisees.

There was nothing here to create a breach between Jesus and the Pharisees. Yet the breach existed, and it became so impossible to heal that it led in the end to the crucifixion.

The explanation for this cannot be found in the first three gospels, those of Matthew, Mark and Luke. It is only in the Fourth Gospel that the difference between Jesus and the Pharisees is made clear, a difference so fundamental that it could not be reconciled.

CHAPTER FOUR

THE religion of first-century Judaism did not concern itself with the nature of God. As Josephus puts it, "The nature of His real being passes knowledge." Instead, it concerned itself with man's relationship to God.

This relationship was primarily a moral one. It was through doing good and being good that a man could find salvation, and there was little of the spirit of curiosity that had distinguished some of the earlier men of Israel. Men like Moses and Elijah had obviously been searching for the nature of reality, but this was not the concern of the men of first-century Judaism.

A set of Jewish scrolls which were recently found on the shores of the Dead Sea speak of the spirit of truth and the spirit of error, but it is clear from the context that these words have been given an ethical meaning. The men of truth seek God by doing "what is good and upright before Him as He commanded through Moses," while the men of error, who do evil, are doomed "to eternal perdition in the fury of the God of vengeance."

To these men, truth meant righteousness and error meant the absence of righteousness.

The men who produced the Dead Sea Scrolls had dedicated themselves to a life of such intense communal virtue that the rigorous laws of the medieval monks seem lax in comparison. Other groups of Jews, such as the Pharisees, were not quite so hard on themselves. But all these Jews would have agreed with Josephus when he defined their fundamental obligation to God. "Him must we worship by the practice of virtue; for that is the most saintly manner of worshiping God."

In the ministry of Jesus, as it is presented by Matthew and Luke, there is this same emphasis on morality. In the Gospel of Luke his teachings on the subject are not organized, but in Matthew they are drawn together in the beautiful discourse that is called the Sermon on the Mount.

The Sermon on the Mount is not a repudiation of Judaism. It is much more nearly a culmination of its highest teachings in the field of morality. What Jesus said about peacefulness and forgiveness and loving one's enemies had already been suggested by great Pharisees like Hillel; and his warnings against love of possessions and outward show would have been agreed to by any good Jewish rabbi. The subject of the Semon on the Mount is "righteousness," (*Matthew* 5:20) and at no point does it contain anything that would contradict the best in first-century Judaism.

This is true of nearly all the teachings of Jesus as they

are recorded in the first three gospels. There is only one
exception, one indication that Jesus did not believe that
his relationship with God depended on personal righteousness; and this is the only point at which Jesus breaks
with orthodox Judaism as far as the first three gospels are
concerned. A man who knelt to him, asking for advice,
called him "Good master," (*Mark* 10:17) and Jesus answered, "Why callest thou me good? There is none good
but one, that is, God." (*Mark* 10:18)

This insistence on the part of Jesus that he possessed
nothing of himself, not even goodness, and that everything belongs to God, does not appear again in the first
three gospels; but it is the foundation stone of the fourth
gospel, the Gospel of John. Throughout the Fourth
Gospel, Jesus is quoted over and over again as saying that
he has no strength, no authority and no power of his
own. "I can of mine own self do nothing." (*John* 5:30)
"I have not spoken on my own authority." (*John* 12:49)
"I do nothing of myself." (*John* 8:28) "The son can do
nothing of himself, but only what he seeth the Father
do." (*John* 5:19)

In the Fourth Gospel, Jesus' relationship to God has
nothing to do with the possession of morality. It has to do
with being the son of God, and the whole of the Gospel of
John is focused on this one point only.

A misunderstanding arose here between Jesus and the
Jews, for they were already teaching the fatherhood of
God. The doctrine cannot be found in the Old Testa-
ment, except for one reference in the Psalms and one in

the prophet Malachi, but since then it had become a familiar idea among the Jews. One of their prayers echoes four times the refrain, "May it be Thy will, O our Father which art in heaven," and a psalm of thanksgiving in the Dead Sea Scrolls reinforces the point in poetry.

Thou art a Father to all the sons of Thy truth.

Any Jew of the first century would have promptly agreed with the statement that a group of Jews made to Jesus: "We have one Father, even God." (*John* 8:41)

According to the Fourth Gospel, this was not what Jesus meant by the fatherhood of God. To the Jews, God was the ultimate source of life, but to Jesus He was the immediate source. As far as Jesus was concerned, this life was not formed in the womb and it was not subject to the laws of birth or of death. "I live because of the Father." (*John* 6:57) It was a relationship so close and so unchanging that nothing could separate the son from the Father. "I and my Father are one." (*John* 10:30)

In the Fourth Gospel, Jesus defines himself as "a man that hath told you the truth." (*John* 8:40) He said over and over again that it was in the name of this truth that he acted, and that his one function was to make it manifest. "For this cause came I into the world, that I should bear witness unto the truth." (*John* 18:37)

The Fourth Gospel makes it clear that Jesus did not believe that this truth he spoke of was available to him alone. Anyone who understood the message he brought could do what he did. "Verily, verily, I say unto you, he that believeth on me, the works that I do shall he do also; and greater works than these shall he do, because I go unto my Father." (*John* 14:12) When Jesus said this, he had already explained what he meant by believing in him. "He that believeth on me, believeth not on me, but on Him that sent me." (*John* 12:44)

In the Fourth Gospel, what Jesus called "the works that I do" are presented as the direct result of the message Jesus brought. All four gospels make it clear that he was able to heal the sick and raise the dead; but the first three gospels, insofar as they explain the matter at all, give the impression that Jesus had been given a supernatural power to defy physical laws. Only in the Fourth Gospel are these acts of Jesus presented as the inevitable result of his message, the message that brought freedom from every form of bondage because it was the truth about God. The acts that Jesus performed would manifestly be impossible to the teacher of morality who is presented in the gospels of Matthew and Luke. They would be quite possible to a man who had found the nature of reality.

It is worth noticing that John is the only writer in the whole of the Bible who gives a definition of the nature of God. It would not occur to an orthodox Jew to define Him. As Josephus said, the nature of God was unknowable. But John had been close enough to Jesus to lose some of his orthodoxy, and he gives three definitions of God. The first is a direct quotation from Jesus: "God is Spirit." (*John* 4:24) The other two come from John's letters, which are so similar in tone to the Fourth Gospel that they were obviously written by the same man. One of these is the definition that is implicit in the discourse at the Last Supper: "God is Love." (*I John* 4:8) The other is a recapitulation of the ministry of Jesus as it looked to the disciple he loved the most: "This then is the message which we have heard of him, and declare unto you, that God is Light, and in Him is no darkness at all." (*I John* 1:5)

This was the truth about God that Jesus had come to bring. God is Light. Therefore, for His sons there could be no darkness, no estrangement and no death. The life that Jesus taught as the result of this relationship was not subject to destruction, and Jesus called it "eternal life." (*John* 17:2)

Again Jesus was misunderstood, for the Jews also taught eternal life. Like the "fatherhood of God," it was a familiar phrase in Judaism and it always meant a life after death. It was the life that would be achieved after the resurrection of the dead on a final Day of the Lord.

Such a doctrine cannot be found in the Old Testament, although it was hinted at in some of the later prophets. In fact, it was still such a new idea in Judaism that the conservative Sadducees did not believe in it. But the influential Pharisees believed in it strongly, and so did the Essenes. It is clearly expressed in the Dead Sea Scrolls, which promise "everlasting joy in the life of eternity" to the righteous, and eternal damnation for sinners.

The first three gospels, those of Matthew, Mark and Luke, show Jesus in agreement with this Jewish doctrine.

There would be a "resurrection of the just" (*Luke* 14:14) and "in the world to come, eternal life." (*Mark* 10:30)

The first three gospels contain only one hint that Jesus was not as orthodox as they make him seem to be. They report an argument he had with a group of Sadducees on the subject of immortality, and in the course of it he said, "He is not a God of the dead, but of the living." (*Luke* 20:38; *Matthew* 22:32; *Mark* 12:27) Luke adds the even more illuminating quotation: "for all men are alive to Him." Since Jesus was speaking to Sadducees, it might be argued that he was merely upholding the doctrine of a future life against men who disbelieved in it, and that he meant nothing more.

In the Fourth Gospel, however, his position is both so unorthodox and so clear that it appalled the Jews who were talking to him. These were not conservative Sadducees. They were men who "believed in him" (*John* 8:30) and who were ready to become his followers. But they disagreed with him so completely about the nature of God that in the end they tried to stone him for blasphemy. As Jesus said, "Ye say, that He is your God; yet ye have not known Him." (*John* 8:54–55)

The argument between Jesus and these Jews reached its climax when Jesus said, "Verily, verily, I say unto you, if a man keep my saying, he shall never see death." (*John* 8:51) The Jews considered this a preposterous statement. They were willing to agree that the righteous would return to life in the resurrection on the Last Day, but this was not what Jesus had said. "Now we know that

thou hast a devil. Abraham is dead, and the prophets; and
thou sayest, 'If a man keep my saying, he shall never taste
of death.' Art thou greater than our father Abraham,
which is dead? And the prophets are dead. Whom makest
thou thyself?" (*John* 8:52–53)

Jesus answered, "Before Abraham was, I am." (*John*
8:58) The life he was talking about was truly eternal,
having neither beginning nor end. It existed wholly in
relation to God, and because of the nature of God it was
not subject to destruction. The God Jesus called Father
was not the God of the dead but of the living, for all men
are alive to Him.

The eternal life that Jesus taught was not something
to be entered through the door of death. It could be
achieved only by understanding God and accepting the
message that Jesus brought. "And this is life eternal, that
they might know Thee the only true God, and Jesus the
Christ whom Thou hast sent." (*John* 17:3)

Jesus refused to accept the authority of death. He
would not even use the word. He was told that the
daughter of a man named Jairus had died and he said to
the mourners, "Weep not; she is not dead, but sleepeth."
(*Luke* 8:52) The people who were there "laughed him to
scorn, knowing that she was dead." (*Luke* 8:53) But Jesus
had a better witness than the evidence of his own eyes
or the conviction of the people who surrounded him. He
took the twelve-year-old by the hand and spoke to her,
and she became a living child.

The same thing happened in the case of Lazarus who

was a close friend of Jesus. Jesus said to his disciples, "Our friend Lazarus sleepeth; but I go, that I may awake him out of sleep." (*John* 11:11) His disciples assured him that all would be well, and he was obliged to use a word that he preferred to avoid. "Then said Jesus unto them plainly, 'Lazarus is dead.' " (*John* 11:14)

The sister of Lazarus went out to meet him, and Jesus said to her, "Thy brother shall rise again." (*John* 11:23) She was a devout Jewess, familiar with the Jewish doctrine of eternal life, and she thought it was this that Jesus meant. "I know that he shall rise again in the resurrection at the last day." (*John* 11:24)

This was not what Jesus meant. He had already proved what he meant in the case of the daughter of Jairus and the son of a widow at Nain, and he was ready to prove it again in the case of Lazarus. "Said I not unto thee, that, if thou wouldest believe, thou shouldest see the glory of God?" (*John* 11:40) Jesus saw that glory where everyone else saw death; and Lazarus, who had been dead for four days, came out of the tomb. "He that was dead came forth, bound hand and foot with graveclothes . . . Jesus saith unto them, 'Loose him, and let him go.' " (*John* 11:44)

It is not strange that the Jews misunderstood Jesus when he spoke of eternal life, since he was using a phrase that was already familiar to them and giving it a new meaning. The same thing was true of his message about the fatherhood of God. He was trying to put new wine into old wineskins, and so revolutionary a doctrine would have been difficult enough to express in any language.

Under the circumstances, John's achievement in the Fourth Gospel becomes even more remarkable. John knew that he could not begin his gospel with the birth of Jesus, as Matthew and Luke had, because Jesus denied birth when he claimed a relationship to God that had neither beginning nor end. On the other hand, John could not do as Mark did and begin with the opening of the ministry, since it was impossible to record what Jesus taught without first making clear who Jesus was.

Therefore John opened the Fourth Gospel in a way that was wholly his own. "In the beginning was the word, and the word was with God, and the word was God." (*John* 1:1) This "word" is the common Greek *logos* that is used in all four of the gospels, and there is no reason to believe that John meant anything complicated by it. He was using it in its ordinary meaning of "communication." Jesus was the communication between God and man, the one way whereby God could be fully known; and "as many as received him, to them gave he power to become the sons of God . . . born not of blood, nor of the will of the flesh, nor of the will of man, but of God." (*John* 1:12–13)

John called Jesus the "only begotten son" (*John* 3:16) and so he remained. Jesus never found anyone who fully shared his conviction that man is not born of the flesh, anyone willing to disbelieve the evidence of his eyes and the voice of his training and capable of accepting a life that was lived only in relation to God. No one but Jesus consecrated himself wholly to his relationship to God. It was this consecration that gave Jesus the right to be called the Messiah, the "anointed one," or, to use the Greek translation of the word, the Christ.

Here again a misunderstanding arose, for Jesus was not the Messiah that the Jews had been expecting.

The doctrine of the coming Messiah took a variety of forms in first-century Judaism, but the most influential view was that of the *Book of Enoch*. Here, the Messiah is presented as a supernatural being, sometimes called the Elect One and sometimes the Son of Man, who will save the whole earth.

He shall be a staff to the righteous. . .
And he shall be the light of the Gentiles,
And the hope of those who are troubled of heart.
All who dwell on earth shall fall down and worship be-
fore him,
And will praise and bless . . . the Lord of Spirits.
And for this reason hath he been chosen and hidden be-
fore Him,
Before the creation of the world and for evermore.
And the wisdom of the Lord of Spirits hath revealed him
to the holy and righteous. . .
For in his name they are saved.

According to the *Book of Enoch,* the Messiah would be set on "a throne of glory" to judge all mankind. The sinners would be destroyed, but the elect would be established "in the light of eternal life."

The righteous and elect will be saved on that day. . .
And the Lord of Spirits will abide over them

And with that Son of Man shall they eat,
And lie down and rise up for ever and ever.

The *Book of Enoch* was eloquently written, and since it was believed to be very ancient it made a profound impression on a great many Jews. Among them was Jude, "the servant of Jesus Christ, and brother of James," (*Jude* 1:1) who quotes from it directly in his epistle in the New Testament. "Enoch also, the seventh from Adam, prophesied of these, saying, 'Behold, the Lord cometh with ten thousand of his saints, to execute judgment upon all.' " (*Jude* 1:14–15)

In each of the three gospels of Matthew, Mark and Luke, the *Book of Enoch* is echoed in descriptions of the Day of Judgment that are attributed to Jesus. This was the time, according to the *Book of Enoch,* when the whole world would see the "Son of Man sitting on the throne of his glory," and the description which is given in each of these three gospels is that of orthodox Judaism.

When the Son of Man shall come in his glory, and all the holy angels with him, then shall he sit upon the throne of his glory: and before him shall be gathered all nations. . . . Then shall the King say unto them on his right hand, "Come, ye blessed of my Father, inherit the kingdom prepared for you from the foundation of the world. . . ." Then shall he say also unto them on the left hand, "Depart from me, ye cursed, into everlasting fire. . . ." And these shall go away into everlasting punishment: but the righteous into life eternal.

(*Matthew* 25:31–32, 34, 41, 46)

It is unquestionably true that Jesus called himself the "son of man," for the term occurs eighty-one times in the four gospels; but that does not mean that he was identifying himself with the supernatural judge of the *Book of Enoch.* There is an older and simpler use of the term in its religious sense, the one that appears nearly ninety times in the Book of Ezekiel in the Old Testament. Whenever God speaks to Ezekiel he calls him "son of man," and that is almost certainly the association that made the term seem important to Jesus. It was the writings of the prophets that Jesus fulfilled, not those of the *Book of Enoch.*

There was one other phrase which Jesus used a great deal and which was also misunderstood by his followers, and that was the kingdom of heaven.

The "kingdom of God" or the "kingdom of heaven" was a familiar idea in first-century Judaism. It described the final state of blessedness that would be ushered in by God and His Messiah, after the righteous had been rewarded and the evil punished. There were differences of opinion about the exact details of the kingdom, but all Jews expected it to take place in the future and to be accompanied by world-wide, visible signs.

The gospels of Matthew, Mark and Luke all echo this conviction and attribute it to Jesus. "There shall be signs in the sun, and in the moon, and in the stars. . . . And then shall they see the Son of Man coming in a cloud with power and great glory." (*Luke* 21:25, 27) Yet Luke records a statement by Jesus which wholly contradicts this Jewish doctrine: "The kingdom of God cometh not with observation: neither shall they say, lo here! or, lo there! for behold, the kingdom of God is within you." (*Luke* 17:20–21)

The Fourth Gospel makes clear what Jesus meant by the kingdom of God. It was not a supernatural event, to be ushered in by angels and clouds of fire during some time in the future. It was an inward kingdom, born of the knowledge of the presence of God. "Verily, verily, I say unto thee, except a man be born . . . of the spirit, he cannot enter into the kingdom of God. That which is born of the flesh is flesh; and that which is born of the spirit is spirit. Marvel not that I said unto thee, ye must be born again." (*John* 3:5–7)

To be born of the spirit meant to be born of God. "God is Spirit: and they that worship Him must worship Him in spirit and in truth." (*John* 4:24) It was to teach this new way of worshiping God that Jesus opened his ministry in Judea. For the Jews believed that the truest worship was "the practice of virtue," and Jesus believed that the truest worship was the understanding of God.

CHAPTER FIVE

ACCORDING to Luke, Jesus began his ministry when he was "about thirty years of age." (*Luke* 3:23) It is not known what he was doing before that time, although there have been various speculations on the subject.

One thing, however, is certain. Jesus must have spent a great deal of time studying the Jewish Scripture. His profound knowledge of what is now called the Old Testament extended even to small details, and he knew some of the writings so well he might almost have learned them by heart.

In itself this was not unusual. What Josephus called "a thorough and accurate" knowledge of the Law was expected of every male Jew, and Josephus himself was so learned that when he was only fourteen the leading men of Jerusalem came to him for information. The whole emphasis of a boy's upbringing was on his knowledge of Scripture, and Jesus was only one of many who were thoroughly grounded in the Law and the prophets.

The difference between Jesus and the others was that he read the Scripture in his own fashion, not with the obedience that took its guidance from those in authority but with the freedom that made him truly a prophet. When a prophet of Israel had made a discovery, he did not present it as the result of tradition. It was never "Thus said our ancestors" or "Thus saith the printed page" but always "Thus saith the Lord." When Jesus began his ministry, it was said of him that he taught "as one that had authority, and not as the scribes," (*Mark* 1:22) and he would allow no man to tell him what to think.

The Jews had a tendency to treat Scripture in the same way that the Christians did later, quoting passages to support positions that had not been held by the original writers. This was so common a device that it was used even by Jesus himself. When he wished to prove that the Christ was not the son of David, he chose an obscure passage from one of the Psalms (*Psalms* 110:1) and reinterpreted it with an ingenuity worthy of any doctor of the Law. (*Matthew* 22:43–45; *Mark* 12:36–37; *Luke* 20:42–44) But he never used the letter of the Old Testament to oppose its spirit.

At the beginning of his ministry Jesus spent forty days in the wilderness, preparing himself to go out among the people of Galilee, and his thoughts were very much with the forty years in the wilderness that Moses described in the Book of Deuteronomy. Three times Jesus was tempted to betray his discovery, and each time he answered with a quotation from Deuteronomy.

Matthew and Luke use the terminology of their own day and describe these temptations as coming from the devil; but all of them were inherent in the fact that Jesus' knowledge of his relationship to God had released him from the bondage of physical law. He was hungry, and why should he not perform a miracle to save himself? "The devil said unto him, 'If thou be the son of God, command this stone that it be made bread.' " (*Luke* 4:3) Jesus answered, "It is written, that man shall not live by bread alone, but by every word of God." (*Luke* 4:4) This is a quotation from the Book of Deuteronomy: "Man doth not live by bread only, but by every word that proceedeth out of the mouth of the Lord." (*Deuteronomy* 8:3)

Then Jesus was tempted to use his power to rule "all the kingdoms of the world" (*Luke* 4:5) and he remembered the warning of Moses, "Thou shalt fear the Lord thy God, and serve Him." (*Deuteronomy* 6:13) "Jesus answered and said unto him, 'Get thee behind me, Satan: for it is written, Thou shalt worship the Lord thy God, and Him only shalt thou serve.' " (*Luke* 4:8)

A third time the temptation came to him, and this time it came in the language of Scripture. (*Luke* 4:10–11) Could he not prove his authority by throwing himself down from some great height and remaining unharmed? For the Lord of Israel has promised perfect safety.

> He shall give His angels charge over thee,
> To keep thee in all thy ways.

They shall bear thee up in their hands,
Lest thou dash thy foot against a stone.

(*Psalms* 91:11–12)

For the third time Jesus answered from Deuteronomy:
"It is said, Thou shalt not tempt the Lord thy God."
(*Luke* 4:12; *Deuteronomy* 6:16)

During the course of his ministry, Jesus was asked to
define the greatest commandment of them all. (*Matthew*
22:36–39) He drew the first part of his answer from the
Book of Deuteronomy: "Thou shalt love the Lord thy
God with all thine heart, and with all thy soul, and with
all thy might." (*Deuteronomy* 6:5) To that he added a
statement attributed to Moses in the Book of Leviticus:
"Thou shalt love thy neighbor as thyself." (*Leviticus*
19:18)

Jesus reached back from the letter of the Old Testament to its spirit, and he read both the Law and the
prophets in the light of that spirit. He quoted directly
from many of the prophets—Hosea, Isaiah, Jeremiah,
Zechariah and Malachi—but it may have been the Psalms
he loved the most, for he turned to them at the crucifixion.

The people of Scripture, men like David and Elijah
and Jonah and Solomon, were as familiar to Jesus as the
people of his own town, and he used them for illustration
as freely as he turned to the flowers of Galilee or to the
details of planting and harvesting that his listeners knew
so well. His knowledge of Scripture was the root and

basis of his ministry, and Israel's greatest prophet never ceased to acknowledge that debt.

It is recorded in the Gospel of Luke that after Jesus returned from the wilderness "he came to Nazareth, where he had been brought up; and, as his custom was, he went into the synagogue on the sabbath day, and stood up to read." (*Luke* 4:16–17) He was given the Book of Isaiah, and he opened it to one of its most beautiful passages. (*Luke* 4:18–19)

> The spirit of the Lord God is upon me;
> Because the Lord hath anointed me
> To preach good tidings unto the afflicted.
> He hath sent me to bind up the broken-hearted,
> To proclaim liberty to the captives,
> And the opening of the prison to them that are bound;
> To proclaim the acceptable year of the Lord.
>
> (*Isaiah* 61:1–2)

The eyes of all the people were fixed on him as he closed the book, gave it back to the attendant and sat down; "and he began to say unto them, 'This day is this scripture fulfilled in your ears.' " (*Luke* 4:21)

It was not what the people of Nazareth had expected. Their meetings in the synagogue had trained them to study the ancient prophets, not to recognize a new one. Moreover, Jesus had been brought up in the town, and the people knew him as a neighbor and not as the fulfillment of prophecy. "Is not this Joseph's son?" (*Luke* 4:22) Jesus himself had not expected them to believe him. "Verily I say unto you, no prophet is accepted in his own country." (*Luke* 4:24)

The first man to give public recognition to Jesus was that very remarkable individual, John the Baptist. The two were kinsmen and had been born only a few months apart. It was to visit John's mother, Elizabeth, that Mary had journeyed from Galilee into the hill country of Judea, and the two women were obviously close friends. It may be that their sons were friends also, but John the Baptist had chosen a different course from Jesus. He retired from the normal world to live like a hermit, dressing in rough skins and leather and eating what grew in the countryside.

Such hermits were not uncommon among the Jews. Josephus spent three years as the disciple of a man "who dwelt in the wilderness, wearing only such clothing as trees provided, feeding on such things as grew of themselves." But John the Baptist was no quiet anchorite. He preached with a vigor that made many people believe that Elijah had returned, as had been promised, and he even dressed like Elijah in a garment of haircloth with a leather girdle.

The ceremony of baptism was already familiar to the Jews, since it was required of all converts to Judaism; but John preached a new "baptism of repentance" (*Mark* 1:4) and applied it to the Jews themselves. He told them they could not expect to find salvation merely because their forefathers had a covenant with God. "Think not to say within yourselves, 'We have Abraham to our father': for I say unto you, that God is able of these stones to raise up children unto Abraham." (*Matthew* 3:9) John was not a traditionalist, and perhaps that is the reason he was the first to recognize Jesus. "I saw and bare record that this is the son of God." (*John* 1:34)

Later on, John the Baptist became less sure of his kinsman. By that time John had been imprisoned by King Herod and could not question Jesus himself, but he sent his disciples to ask if Jesus were the promised Messiah. "Art thou he that should come, or do we look for another?" (*Matthew* 11:3) Jesus replied, "Go and show John again those things which ye do hear and see: the blind receive their sight, and the lame walk, the lepers are cleansed, and the deaf hear, the dead are raised up." (*Matthew* 11:4–5)

It had always been the test of a prophet in Israel that he could prove what he said. If he could do that, he spoke in the name of the Lord; if not, he was a false prophet. Moses said that if anyone asked the question: "How shall we know the word which the Lord hath not spoken?" the answer was this: "When a prophet speaketh in the name of the Lord, if the thing follow not, nor come to pass, that is the thing which the Lord hath not spoken." (*Deuteronomy* 18:21–22)

When Jesus said to a crippled woman, "Thou art loosed from thine infirmity," (*Luke* 13:12) he spoke in the name of the Lord; and because he spoke truly, "immediately she was made straight." (*Luke* 13:13) His authority as a prophet lay in the fact that he could prove what he said, and he took Isaiah's great words to himself because he had a right to them. He brought liberty to the captives and the opening of their prison to those who were in bondage, not through his own authority but through his knowledge of God. "Ye shall know the truth, and the truth shall make you free." (*John* 8:32)

John the Baptist was a man of great influence in both Judea and Galilee, but Jesus did not need John as a witness. "I have greater witness than that of John: for the works which the Father hath given me to finish, the same works that I do, bear witness of me, that the Father hath sent me." (*John* 5:36)

These works are described over and over again, and in great detail, in all four of the gospels. The father of a dying child came to Jesus, and a paralytic who had to be lowered from overhead because the crowds were so great. Lepers came to him and cripples, the deaf, the diseased, and the insane, and he freed them all. "Great multitudes came unto him, having with them those that were lame, blind, dumb, maimed, and many others, and cast them down at Jesus' feet; and he healed them." (*Matthew* 15:30) He "went about all Galilee, teaching in their synagogues, and preaching the gospel of the kingdom, and healing all manner of sickness and all manner of disease among the people. And his fame went throughout all Syria; and they brought unto him all sick people that were taken with divers diseases and torments, and those which were possessed with devils, and those which were lunatic, and those that had the palsy; and he healed them." (*Matthew* 4:23–24)

Once, when Jesus healed a leper, he asked him to tell no one. "But so much the more went there a fame abroad of him; and great multitudes came together to hear, and to be healed by him of their infirmities. And he withdrew himself into the wilderness, and prayed." (*Luke* 5:15–16)

There was a heavy pressure on Jesus to glorify himself rather than the message he brought, the same pressure he had known in the original temptation in the wilderness. He never consented to it. He held to one thing only, his own relationship to God. "When he had sent the multitudes away, he went up into a mountain apart to pray." (*Matthew* 14:23) "In the morning, rising up a great while before day, he went out, and departed into a solitary place, and there prayed." (*Mark* 1:35) "He sent away the people. And when he had sent them away, he departed into a mountain to pray." (*Mark* 6:45–46) "He went out into a mountain to pray, and continued all night in prayer to God." (*Luke* 6:12)

This quality of consecration, of absolute dedication to one thing only, was the quality that Jesus demanded also of his followers. The kingdom of heaven was not something to be put on top of ordinary living, so that only a few minor adjustments were necessary. On the contrary, it swept away everything that had been believed before and required a wholly new way of looking at things. John the Baptist said, "Repent," a word that meant literally, "Change your minds," but this was not enough. A rebirth was required, so that life was lived on an entirely new basis. "Verily, verily, I say unto thee, except a man be born again, he cannot see the kingdom of God." (*John* 3:3)

Jesus described the kingdom of heaven in a parable as being like a treasure hidden in a field. The man who finds it, "for joy thereof goeth and selleth all that he hath, and buyeth that field." (*Matthew* 13:44) Nothing was asked in return except the insistent desire that in itself is prayer. "I say unto you, ask, and it shall be given you; seek, and ye shall find; knock, and it shall be opened unto you." (*Luke* 11:9) What Jesus called "the spirit of truth, which proceedeth from the Father" (*John* 15:26) was available to anyone who was capable of receiving it. As Jesus said, even a human father gives gifts to his son. "How much more shall your heavenly Father give the holy spirit to them that ask Him." (*Luke* 11:13)

Since Jesus claimed nothing for himself, the authority with which he spoke was not his own either. "My doctrine is not mine, but His that sent me. If any man will do His will, he shall know of the doctrine, whether it be of God, or whether I speak of myself. He that speaketh of himself seeketh his own glory; but he that seeketh His glory that sent him, the same is true." (*John* 7:16–18)

In the first three gospels, when Jesus was asked by what authority he spoke, he refused to answer, (*Luke* 20:8; *Matthew* 21:27; *Mark* 11:33) although he did give a parable about a son who had done his father's will. In the Gospel of John, however, Jesus stated very clearly and many times on what authority he acted, an authority that was unshakable because it was not his own.

Luke tells the story of a Roman military commander who asked some of the Jewish leaders in the community to intercede for him with Jesus. Since he had built their synagogue for them, they owed him some return, and a servant whom he loved was dying. When Jesus arrived at the house, the Roman sent word that there was no need to come in. "Lord, trouble not thyself. For I am not worthy that thou shouldest enter under my roof; wherefore neither thought I myself worthy to come unto thee; but say in a word, and my servant shall be healed. For I also am a man set under authority, having under me soldiers, and I say unto one, Go, and he goeth; and to another, Come, and he cometh; and to my servant, Do this, and he doeth it." (*Luke* 7:6–8) As a military commander, accustomed to strict obedience, the Roman knew authority when he saw it; and before his messengers had returned to the house, the servant had recovered.

This same instant recognition of authority is evident in the way Jesus chose his disciples. Whatever they may have been doing, he spoke to them and they came. The two brothers, John and James, were mending nets in their father's fishing boat when he called to them, "and they immediately left the ship and their father, and followed him." (*Matthew* 4:22) A man named Matthew had a responsible post in the customs office at Capernaum.

Jesus said to him, " 'Follow me.' And he arose, and followed him." (*Matthew* 9:9)

Nearly all the men whom Jesus chose as his disciples came from Galilee. The one possible exception was Judas Iscariot, whose surname apparently means "of Kerioth." Kerioth was in Judea, and the people of Judea had a tendency to look down on the Galileans. One of the arguments against Jesus when he taught in Jerusalem was that he came from the north. "Out of Galilee ariseth no prophet." (*John* 7:52) The pronunciation of the men of Galilee was a little faulty and indistinct, so that they were not permitted to read public prayers, and Peter was immediately recognized in Judea as a follower of the prophet from Galilee because of his manner of speaking.

Among the Galileans themselves there were levels of respectability. A man who came from the town of Bethsaida found it difficult to believe that Jesus could be the Messiah, in view of the place of his origin. "Can there any good thing come out of Nazareth?" (*John* 1:46) His friend said merely, "Come and see," and when the man from Bethsaida had spoken with Jesus he forgot all his prejudices. "Rabbi, thou art the son of God." (*John* 1:49)

At least half of Jesus' disciples lived along the western shore of the Sea of Galilee. It was also called the Sea of Tiberias or the Sea of Gennesaret, but it was actually an inland lake, fourteen miles long and seven wide. Along its western shore was the most thickly populated area in Galilee, and Josephus, who loved the whole country, said that this was the "best part" of it. It was a beautiful district, heavily under cultivation. Walnuts and figs and grapes flourished the whole year around, and the climate was warm enough even for palm trees.

The beaches of the Sea of Galilee were clean and sandy, and the bright blue water was excellent for drinking. The River Jordan entered at the north end of the lake and flowed through its entire length, so that there was a constant supply of fresh water and excellent drainage, and fish could be found there unlike any others in Palestine. The catch was salted and sold abroad, and the towns and villages that encircled the lake were inhabited mostly by fishermen. When James and John worked in their father's boat his hired servants worked with them, and the fishing industry obviously supported a large number of people. The only drawback was the threat of sudden storms, which were born in the surrounding hills and came without warning.

The eastern shore of the lake was not in Galilee, and the upper section of it lay in the realm of King Philip. He was another of the many sons of Herod the Great, and Jesus frequently visited his capital city of Julias. Philip had turned it into a Greek city and named it in honor of the daughter of a Roman er .peror, but the inhabitants of the Jewish quarter still clung to its old name, Bethsaida. It was in this city that Jesus healed a blind man and fed a multitude with five loaves and two fishes. There was also a town of that name in Galilee, and three of his disciples came from there.

When Jesus taught in Galilee he usually made his

headquarters in Capernaum, at the northern end of the lake. Jesus paid his temple tax at Capernaum, and when he returned there after a journey "it was reported that he was at home." (*Mark* 2:1) Until the new capital of Tiberias had been built farther south on the lake, Capernaum was an important commercial center, and it still had its own customs office and a busy trade in fruit and fish.

There is no record that Jesus ever went to Tiberias, although it was only a few miles from Capernaum. It was a city populated by Gentiles, and the message that Jesus brought was for the Jews. He was willing to teach anywhere, on the shore of the Lake of Galilee or even from a boat, but the most natural place was in each case the local synagogue. Jesus taught in the synagogues of Nazareth and Capernaum and in those of the towns and villages wherever he went, and in Jerusalem he taught in the Temple. He specifically instructed his disciples, "Go not into the way of the Gentiles." (*Matthew* 10:5) It was only the Jews, the people of the Scripture, who were trained to understand his message, and it was to the Jews that Jesus addressed himself.

Nevertheless, he made no effort to please his fellow countrymen, and in particular he refused to placate the somewhat self-righteous sense of exclusiveness that had kept the Jews intact as a nation. The Jews, for instance, had no dealings with the people of Samaria, nursing a feud that went back to the days when the Temple was rebuilt after the Babylonian Exile. In the eyes of the

Jews the Samaritans were an inferior race, and it was considered legitimate to treat them with loathing and contempt.

Jesus once told a parable to illustrate what he thought of the Jews' attitude toward the Samaritans. A man was on his way to the winter resort of Jericho in Judea when he was attacked by robbers who left him half dead. Two of the purest of Jews racially, a priest and a Levite, passed by without helping him, but a man from the despised race of the Samaritans "had compassion on him" (*Luke* 10:33) and cared for him as though he were a brother.

Jesus once healed ten lepers, and, as he pointed out, the only one who returned to thank him was a Samaritan. "Where are the nine? Was no one found to return and give praise to God, except this stranger?" (*Luke* 17:17–18) The Samaritans rejected the books of the prophets and refused to worship in the Temple, and Jesus made it clear that he did not sympathize with their religious views. He said to a woman of Samaria, "Ye worship ye know not what; we know what we worship: for salvation is of the Jews." (*John* 4:22) But he refused to condemn anyone because of his race.

Nor would Jesus condemn anyone because of his occupation, as he showed in his attitude toward the tax collectors. No one likes to pay taxes; but the Jews had an almost passionate hatred of tax collectors as the living symbol of their subjection to Rome. They gladly paid their half shekel for the upkeep of the Temple, but it was a different matter to be forced to pay tribute to a heathen conqueror.

From the Roman point of view the tax system in the provinces was a sound business measure and, in fact, the chief reason why the provinces existed. The emperor Augustus was the grandson of a banker, and he set up a financial system which most of the provinces managed to endure; but the Jews never resigned themselves either to the weight of the taxes or to the principle behind them. The silver Roman coins in which the taxes were paid bore the image of the current emperor, Tiberius, which broke the second commandment, and they carried an inscription identifying him as the son of a deified Augustus, which broke the first. (*Exodus* 20:3–4)

One kind of taxation—sales taxes, customs payments and so on—was called *publicum* since it was exacted from the general public; and the agents who collected it were called publicans. Their fellow Jews treated them like members of the criminal class and they were shocked that Jesus was willing to dine with so many of them. Jesus knew that he was considered "a friend of publicans and sinners," (*Matthew* 11:19) but the matter did not trouble him.

The one sin that Jesus really attacked was self-righteousness, and this happened to be the besetting sin of a great many of his countrymen. The Jews were so sure, and justifiably, that they were a people set apart from all others that they forgot the virtue of humility; and because they were good men, and knew it, they forgot that righteousness was not the whole of the Law. Jesus once told a parable to illustrate this point. "Two men went up into the temple to pray; the one a Pharisee, and the other a publican. The Pharisee stood and prayed thus with himself, 'God, I thank Thee, that I am not as other men are, extortioners, unjust, adulterers, or even as this publican. I fast twice in the week, I give tithes of all that I possess.' And the publican, standing afar off, would not lift up so much as his eyes unto heaven, but smote upon his breast, saying, 'God be merciful to me a sinner.' " (*Luke* 18:10–13)

It was not that Jesus was opposed to righteousness. But it is hard for a good man to give up his private sense of virtue, as hard as for a rich man to give up his possessions, and everything must be given up in order to enter the kingdom of heaven. It was because the sinner has no pride in his own virtue that Jesus said, "Verily, I say unto you, that the publicans and the harlots go into the kingdom of God before you." (*Matthew* 21:31)

The Pharisees clung to their goodness, holding it so tightly that they could not let it go, and the Essenes valued theirs so much that they withdrew from the world to protect it. But Jesus said of himself, "Why callest thou me good? None is good save one, that is, God." (*Luke* 18:19) And having given everything to God, keeping back nothing for himself, he walked as the only free man in Israel.

CHAPTER SIX

IF Jesus had remained in Galilee and contented himself with teaching in the local synagogues, the authorities might have been spared the necessity of taking action against him. But he came into Judea and taught in the Temple, and the men who governed the country could not ignore the problem he presented.

Judea was ruled as a Roman province, and the authority was vested in a Roman governor named Pontius Pilate. However, it was the policy of the Romans to work through local institutions as far as possible, and they had permitted the Jews to keep their own governing council. It was called the Sanhedrin and was much more powerful under the Romans than it had been under Herod the Great. It consisted of seventy-one members, and while it had no power to impose the death sentence, it had general control over the internal affairs of Judea.

The council maintained its own police force and had the right to make arrests, but its greatest authority lay in the fact that it was the religious as well as the civil guardian of the nation. At its head was the high priest, who traced his descent from Aaron, the brother of Moses.

When the high priest entered the inmost room of the Temple, in his vestments of gold and blue and scarlet and purple and his breastplate adorned with precious stones, he symbolized the relationship of the nation to its one real ruler, the God of Israel.

The capital of Judea was Caesarea, where Pontius Pilate had his official residence, but no Jew looked upon that heathen city by the sea as the source of his government. His real capital was Jerusalem, the holy city, the heart and center of the country, and it was from Jerusalem that the council governed the people of Judea.

The council had a difficult task, for it bore full responsibility for the political and spiritual safety of the nation. On the one side was the tinder-box emotionalism of the people, expecting almost hourly a Messiah who would release them from bondage. On the other side were the occupation forces of the Roman Empire, ready to turn the full weight of its military machine on the unruly third-rate province of Judea if it showed signs of getting out of control.

When the council called a meeting to discuss the problem of Jesus of Nazareth, its members were well aware of what would happen if the current popular excitement over the prophet from Galilee got out of hand. "The Romans shall come and destroy both our place and our nation." (*John* 11:48) This was no imaginary danger. In less than half a century it was precisely what happened: the Jews became uncontrollable, and the

Romans destroyed the city of Jerusalem and every synagogue in Palestine.

It was the business of the council to protect Judea
from danger without and within, from the Romans and
from heresy; and a false Messiah would threaten the
nation on both counts. The council was obliged to consider the welfare of the nation before that of the individual, and Caiaphas, the high priest, was voicing what
must have seemed a very reasonable point of view when
he told his fellow members, "It is expedient for us, that
one man should die for the people, and that the whole
nation perish not." (*John* 11:50)

All Jews were trained to a sense of responsibility for
the community. As Josephus said, "Prayers for the welfare
of the community must take precedence of those for
ourselves." Any Jew would think first of the welfare
of the nation as a whole; and the men of the council,
by virtue of their office, held this position more strongly
than any.

This was not the first time the problem of a false
Messiah had arisen. Such men remained a constant
difficulty, and conservatives like Josephus mistrusted
them. "Impostors and deceivers persuaded the multitude
to follow them into the wilderness and pretended that
they would exhibit manifest wonders and signs that
should be performed by the providence of God." Josephus
singles out one agitator in particular, who came from
Egypt and who persuaded "the multitude of the common
people" to follow him to the Mount of Olives. Most of

these men were executed. It was the only way to keep order in a country already torn by riots, with peace and stability so precarious that even the unworldly Essenes were obliged to carry swords.

The case of Jesus, however, presented a special problem. For he had healed the sick and raised the dead, and it was very difficult to convince the people that he was an impostor. "When Christ cometh, will he do more miracles than these which this man hath done?" (*John* 7:31) The Jewish authorities in Jerusalem had a long argument with a man on the subject and could not shake him; for the man had been blind since birth, and Jesus had healed him. "Since the world began it was not heard that any man opened the eyes of one that was born blind. If this man were not of God, he could do nothing." (*John* 9:32–33)

Opinion among the Jews was sharply divided. "Many of them said, 'He hath a devil, and is mad; why hear ye him?' Others said, 'These are not the words of him that hath a devil. Can a devil open the eyes of the blind?'" (*John* 10:20–21) This same difference of opinion was reflected in the council itself, and it was not a united organization that finally moved against Jesus.

The first three gospels mention only one dissenting member, a rich man named Joseph from the nearby town of Arimathea. The Fourth Gospel, however, makes it clear that there were others. John makes special mention of a Pharisee on the council whose name was Nicodemus; he visited Jesus secretly at the beginning of his ministry and took his part openly when the council wanted to condemn Jesus without a hearing. "Doth our law judge any man, before it hear him?" (*John* 7:51) John also makes it clear that other prominent men would have spoken for Jesus if they dared. "Among the chief rulers also many believed on him; but . . . they did not confess him, lest they should be put out of the synagogue." (*John* 12:42) One of the most feared forms of excommunication was exclusion from the synagogue, since it cut the victim off from nearly all intercourse with his fellow Jews.

The Jewish authorities were willing to use any weapon at their disposal to punish those who tried to break away from the will of the majority. Discipline of this kind held the nation together against the recurring pressures that might otherwise have made it crumble and fall apart, and the council believed that in the rigidity of the Law lay its strength.

Jesus once said, "Think not that I am come to destroy the law, or the prophets; I am not come to destroy, but to fulfill." (*Matthew* 5:17) He obeyed the Law in matters of ceremony and was faithful to its spirit, but in one sense at least he was not a good Jew. He would not bow to accredited authority.

This had been true of all the great prophets of Israel. The only authority they would accept came direct from God, and from the point of view of the community nearly all of them had been troublemakers.

Until Jesus came, the most iconoclastic of the prophets

had been Jeremiah. He stood at the gates of the Temple and bluntly told the people that what their leaders believed to be the truth was in fact "the deceit of their own heart." (*Jeremiah* 23:26) In return he was bitterly accused of misleading the people. There was more than one attempt to kill Jeremiah, and a prophet named Uriah who brought a similar message was murdered.

It was not because they failed in their love of God that the Jews persecuted their greatest prophets; it was because they clung too narrowly to their own sense of truth. Like the priests who opposed Jeremiah, the council members who opposed Jesus were good men. They were convinced that they already possessed the full truth about God, to which nothing could be added; and when Jesus presented his own discovery to the people, they could not see that this was the illumination that had been promised. They saw it as blasphemy. Between goodness and greatness there is often no bridge at all, and when good men are mindful of their responsibility to the community they will sometimes strike out at a savior because he seems to them to be a destroyer.

The majority of the men on the council believed that Jesus was a troublemaker who was threatening the peace of Israel by misleading the people. Some of them had misgivings. But Caiaphas, the high priest, was convinced that Jesus must be executed, and he managed to persuade the others that there was only one correct way of looking at the problem: it was better for one man to die, even

though he might be innocent, than for the whole nation
to be destroyed.

As for Jesus himself, his warfare was not with the
Jewish council; he was not fighting anything so transitory.
The enemy he challenged was greater than Jerusalem,
and greater even than the power of Rome. For Jesus was
challenging death. He had undertaken to prove that death
had no power over the son of God.

Jesus followed with open eyes the path that led to the
crucifixion, and he said over and over again that he submitted to it voluntarily. "I lay down my life, that I might
take it again. No man taketh it from me, but I lay it
down of myself. I have power to lay it down, and I have
power to take it again. This commandment have I received of my Father." (*John* 10:17–18)

If Jesus had been willing to stay out of Judea, he would
not have been subject to the actions of the council. Instead, he returned, and the specific event that brought him
back was the death of Lazarus. Lazarus lived in Bethany,
a town about two miles east of Jerusalem, and when
Jesus' disciples failed in their effort to persuade him not
to return to Judea, they decided to go back with him.
"Let us also go, that we may die with him." (*John* 11:16)

Jesus himself was not concerned with death, however
bravely faced. He was concerned with life. He stood in
front of the tomb of his friend at Bethany, and he thanked
God for what he saw when everyone else saw death.
"Father, I thank Thee that Thou hast heard me. And I
knew that Thou hearest me always." (*John* 11:41–42)

Then he said in a loud voice, "Lazarus, come forth," (*John* 11:43) and Lazarus came.

A meeting of the council was called as soon as the news of this reached Jerusalem. "Then gathered the chief priests and the Pharisees a council, and said, 'What do we? For this man doeth many miracles. And if we let him thus alone, all men will believe on him.'" (*John* 11:47–48) It was decided that a way must be found to arrange his execution, and "from that day forth they took counsel together for to put him to death." (*John* 11:53)

Jesus went for a time to a town about eight miles away. Then he returned to Bethany and attracted a large crowd by his presence. There were an enormous number of people in and around Jerusalem in any case, for the feast of the Passover was only six days away.

From all over Palestine and from all the neighboring nations, the Jews gathered by tens of thousands for the festival in the holy city, and Josephus describes the annual influx of pilgrims as an "innumerable multitude." They were in a high state of religious excitement when they flocked into the already crowded city, and the Roman governor took his usual precautions. Pilate left his capital city on the seacoast and came to Jerusalem for the seven days of the festival. He took up residence in the palace that had been built by Herod the Great and had since been turned into an army barracks, and he stationed guards by the galleries surrounding the Temple. There was always a danger of riots in Jerusalem and they were never more likely to occur than during the week of

Passover, when the Jews were celebrating an earlier de-
liverance from bondage.

Jesus was well aware that some of the people believed
he was a political savior who would free them from the
Romans. To make it clear that he was not, he used an
old prophetic device—the visual acting-out of a message.
Jeremiah had hidden a linen cloth in the cleft of a rock
and Ezekiel had dug through a wall with baggage on his
shoulder, both of them using a kind of visible parable
to make their meanings clear; and Jesus used the same
device to show the people the nature of his ministry.

In their excitement, the people welcomed him into
Jerusalem as though he were a king. They "took branches
of palm trees, and went forth to meet him, and cried,
'Hosanna! Blessed is the king of Israel that cometh in
the name of the Lord.' " (*John* 12:13) Jesus found a young
ass and sat upon it, acting out a passage from Scripture
which any good Jew would recognize at once.

> Shout, O daughter of Jerusalem!
> Behold, thy king cometh unto thee:
> He is just, and having salvation;
> Lowly, and riding upon an ass.
>
> (*Zechariah* 9:9)

Jesus had not come as a political conqueror. As he later
told Pilate, his kingdom was "not of this world," (*John*
18:36) and the salvation he brought was not freedom
from the dominion of Rome.

The story is told a little differently in the other three
gospels, where it sounds as though the entrance into

Jerusalem had been planned by Jesus himself. In this, as in so much else, the first three gospels seem to be less reliable. Even the cry of the people as it is recorded in Matthew and Mark is a curious one. According to John, they shouted "Hosanna," which means, "Oh, save." According to Matthew and Mark, they shouted "Hosanna in the highest," (*Matthew* 21:9; *Mark* 11:10) which is meaningless.

The usual time for the Jews to carry palm branches was at the Feast of the Tabernacles, testifying to their victory over the heathen, and it was perhaps in that sense that the people carried them before Jesus when he entered Jerusalem. But the battle in which he was engaged did not concern any human enemy, and only the Gospel of John shows the nature of the battle. "Now is my soul troubled; and what shall I say? 'Father, save me from this hour'? But for this cause came I unto this hour. Father, glorify Thy name." (*John* 12:27–28)

A short time earlier Jesus had stood in front of the tomb of Lazarus, surrounded by the Jews who were mourning the death of his friend, and had demanded, "Said I not unto thee, that, if thou wouldest believe, thou shouldest see the glory of God?" (*John* 11:40) Now he was prepared to offer the final evidence of that glory, and he submitted to the test in the holy city. For, as he himself said, "It cannot be that a prophet should perish away from Jerusalem." (*Luke* 13:33)

CHAPTER SEVEN

ON the evening before his crucifixion, Jesus met with his disciples in an upstairs room in Jerusalem to partake of the Last Supper. According to the first three gospels, this was the Passover supper, the highly ceremonial meal that took place at sundown as the Passover began. According to the Fourth Gospel it was not the Passover supper and took place twenty-four hours earlier.

The Passover supper marked the opening of the seven days of Passover, symbolizing the departure of the children of Israel from Egypt, and the ritual of the meal was ancient and undeviating. If the Last Supper was the Passover supper, the meat the disciples ate was the sacrificial lamb that Moses had commanded, the lamb "without blemish." (*Exodus* 12:5) The bread that Jesus broke was unleavened bread, "the bread of affliction," (*Deuteronomy* 16:3) and the hymn they all sang at the end was the "hallel," the selection from the Book of Psalms that always closed the meal. Jesus extended the symbolism of the occasion by saying that the bread they ate was his body and the wine they drank was his blood. Then he went

out to the Mount of Olives, and there he was arrested, to
be crucified. Since the Jewish day began at sundown, it
was therefore still the first day of Passover when Jesus was
tried, executed and buried.

Matthew, Mark and Luke agree on this dating, but
they also agree on a series of events that are impossible to
reconcile with such a date. The first and seventh days
of Passover were very strictly observed by all Jews, and
they were surrounded by a series of ritualistic prohibi-
tions. For instance, the carrying of weapons was forbidden on the first day of Passover. Yet Matthew, Mark
and Luke all agree that the men who were sent by the
Jewish council to arrest Jesus came armed "with swords
and staves" (*Matthew* 26:47; *Mark* 14:43; *Luke* 22:52)
and that some of the disciples were also armed.

According to Matthew and Mark, the council had defi-
nitely decided not to arrest Jesus during the Passover,
"lest there be an uproar among the people." (*Matthew*
26:5; *Mark* 14:2) This was one additional objection to an
act that would have involved the council in a series of
violations of the Law.

On the other hand, Matthew, Mark and Luke had a
good reason for wishing to perpetuate the tradition that
the Last Supper was a Passover supper. It made it possible for the early Christians to press the relationship between the sacrifice of an unblemished lamb on the first
day of Passover and the sacrifice of Jesus on the cross. One
of the epistles of Peter in the New Testament draws a
specific connection between "the precious blood of

Christ" and that of "a lamb without blemish." (*I Peter* 1:19)

John was certainly aware of this symbolism also, and twice in the Fourth Gospel Jesus is called "the lamb of God." (*John* 1:29, 36) Nevertheless, according to the Gospel of John, the Last Supper took place twenty-four hours before the Passover began. The great haste showed by the Jewish authorities throughout the trial and execution is explained by John as an attempt to have everything finished before sundown; "for that sabbath day was an high day." (*John* 19:31) In that particular year, the seventh day of the week coincided with the first day of the Passover.

The Fourth Gospel, unlike the other three, shows no inconsistency here, and even the smallest details reinforce the dating. For instance, John reports that at the end of the Last Supper Jesus said to Judas Iscariot, "That thou doest, do quickly." (*John* 13:27) Judas was treasurer for the group and carried the money bag, and some of the disciples concluded that Judas was being sent out to make the complicated arrangements for the Passover supper. "Some of them thought, because Judas had the bag, that Jesus had said unto him, 'Buy those things that we have need of for the feast.' " (*John* 13:29)

In one sense it does not matter whether the Last Supper took place twenty-four hours before the feast of the Passover, as John says, or whether it took place on the evening of the Passover, as the other three gospels say it did; the question of the exact date is not of vital im-

portance. In another sense, however, the discrepancy matters a great deal, since it involves the question of the
reliability of the Fourth Gospel. In this gospel there is a
long account of what Jesus told his followers that night,
a discourse that does not appear in Matthew, Mark or
Luke. If John is a trustworthy witness on the other details connected with the Last Supper, it seems reasonable
to suppose that he can be trusted in this also.

The first three gospels give relatively little space to
what Jesus said that night, but at one point there is a
promise to his disciples that is almost a direct echo of
the *Book of Enoch*. "I appoint unto you a kingdom, as
my Father hath appointed unto me; that ye may eat and
drink at my table in my kingdom, and sit on thrones judg-
ing the twelve tribes of Israel." (*Luke* 22:29–30) This
may very well have been what his disciples were hoping
for, but it is not very likely that this is what Jesus promised them. He was not the Messiah of Jewish orthodoxy.

When John wrote the Fourth Gospel, he had two ad-
vantages over Matthew, Mark and Luke. He was better
informed about the actual Jewish background of the
events he was describing, and at the same time he was
much less influenced by orthodox Judaism. John was
himself a Jew, and he could not release himself wholly
from his training; but at least he was able to free himself sufficiently to hear what Jesus was really saying on
the evening of the Last Supper.

Jesus began his discourse to his disciples as soon as
Judas Iscariot had left the room to betray him to the

authorities. "It was night," (*John* 13:30) but there was a light in the room that had no dependence on the sun.

"Now is the son of man glorified, and God is glorified in him . . . Little children, yet a little while I am with you. Ye shall seek me; and as I said unto the Jews so now I say unto you, Whither I go ye cannot come. A new commandment I give unto you, that ye love one another; as I have loved you, that ye also love one another." (*John* 13:31, 33–34)

Peter loved Jesus with the whole force of his passionate nature, and Peter demanded, "Why cannot I follow thee now? I will lay down my life for thy sake." (*John* 13:37) It was Jesus to whom Peter clung, not to the truth that Jesus brought, and Jesus knew exactly how trustworthy that kind of love would prove to be. "Wilt thou lay down thy life for my sake? Verily, verily, I say unto thee, the cock shall not crow, till thou hast denied me thrice." (*John* 13:38)

Jesus knew that when his disciples watched the arrest, and then the crucifixion, they would forget everything he had told them. When he was nailed to the cross, they would believe in the nails. They had never really understood the message he brought; they had only understood what he was able to do as the result of the message, and when he did nothing to save himself they would no longer be able to believe in him.

The temptation to stay with them and go on teaching must have been very great. But throughout the whole of

his ministry Jesus had held to nothing except his knowledge of God, letting everything else go, and in the end he
let go even his final desire to protect the men he loved.
He left them instead to the spirit of truth, which could
be the only real protection. "I will pray the Father, and
He shall give you another comforter, that he may abide
with you forever; even the spirit of truth." (*John* 14:
16–17) "The comforter, which is the holy spirit, whom
the Father will send in my name, he shall teach you
all things." (*John* 14:26)

The word that is given here as "comforter" has also
been translated as "helper" or "counselor." The Greek
word is *paraclete,* and the literal translation would be:
"one called alongside." It is a word that appears no-
where in the New Testament except in this discourse that
is recorded by John.

This was the force that Jesus trusted, the impersonal
truth, the fact that it is so. It was not possible for his
disciples to turn to it as long as they could turn to him
instead. "I tell you the truth; it is expedient for you that
I go away: for if I go not away, the comforter will not
come unto you . . . When he, the spirit of truth, is
come, he will guide you into all truth." (*John* 16: 7, 13)

From the beginning of his ministry, Jesus had found
that many men would rather believe in him than in the
message he brought. He gave honor to God; they tried
to give honor to him instead. Once, a man whom he had
healed asked to be permitted to become his follower.

"Jesus sent him away, saying, 'Return to thine own house, and show how great things God hath done unto thee.' And he went his way, and proclaimed throughout the whole city how great things Jesus had done unto him." (*Luke* 8: 38–39) This was not what Jesus had told him to do. He never asked for personal glorification or personal praise, and it was not some private power of his own that he wanted his disciples to trust. "The word which ye hear is not mine, but the Father's which sent me." (*John* 14:24)

There was no need for his disciples to be frightened, if only they would trust the spirit of truth that Jesus himself trusted. "Peace I leave with you, my peace I give unto you: not as the world giveth, give I unto you. Let not your heart be troubled, neither let it be afraid. Ye have heard how I said unto you, I go away, and come again unto you. If ye loved me, ye would rejoice, because I said, I go unto the Father: for my Father is greater than I . . . That the world may know that I love the Father, and as the Father gave me commandment, even so I do." (*John* 14: 27–28; 31)

It was love that Jesus was talking about in the whole of his discourse; and, as John said later in one of his letters, "There is no fear in love; but perfect love casteth out fear." (*I John* 4:18) It was this love that Jesus offered to his frightened disciples. "As the Father hath loved me, so have I loved you; continue ye in my love. If ye keep my commandments, ye shall abide in my love; even as I have kept my Father's commandments, and abide in His love. These things have I spoken unto you, that my joy might remain in you, and that your joy might be full." (*John* 15: 9–11)

It was like Jesus to describe his ministry in such terms. It could not have failed to be happy; for he knew what he trusted, and his trust was complete.

On one occasion during his ministry, his disciples had tried in vain to heal a boy who was an epileptic, and Jesus had healed him at once. He told his disciples that they had failed because they expected to fail. "For verily I say unto you, if ye have faith as a grain of mustard seed, ye shall say unto this mountain, 'Remove hence to yonder place,' and it shall remove; and nothing shall be impossible unto you." (*Matthew* 17:20) It was easy for the disciples to have faith as long as they had the evidence of their own eyes and the excitement of the healings to support them. It would not be so easy when all this was lacking.

Jesus knew that if he did nothing to prevent his own death his disciples would forsake him. Yet even that left him untroubled. "Ye shall be scattered, every man to his own, and shall leave me alone; and yet I am not alone, because the Father is with me." (*John* 16:32)

Jesus turned from his disciples then and prayed directly to God. "Father, the hour is come." (*John* 17:1) He prayed for the safety of the men he loved, and once again he spoke of his happiness. "I come to Thee; and these things I speak in the world, that they might have my joy fulfilled in themselves . . . Sanctify them through Thy truth: Thy word is truth." (*John* 17:13, 17) "O righteous Father, the world hath not known Thee; but I have known Thee, and these have known that Thou hast sent me. And I have declared unto them Thy name, and will declare it: that the love wherewith Thou hast loved me may be in them, and I in them." (*John* 17:25–26)

With that he ceased speaking. He left Jerusalem with his disciples and went to a garden about a mile beyond the city walls. The garden was named Gethsemane, and Jesus visited it often. It was there that Judas betrayed him to the authorities.

The first three gospels record that while Jesus was in Gethsemane he prayed "in an agony" (*Luke* 22:44) that he should be spared the crucifixion. But they also record that all his disciples were sleeping, and it is difficult to see how they could have heard what he said.

If the ministry of Jesus had come to a close with his death on the cross, it would be legitimate to mistrust the Fourth Gospel. The serenity and strength which Jesus shows in the Gospel of John would be impossible, and John would be a misleading witness. But all four gospels unite to say that the ministry of Jesus did not end with the crucifixion.

Jesus opened his ministry in Nazareth with a quotation from the Book of Isaiah. Now, in Jerusalem, and in the name of the truth that he served, he was about to fulfill another prophecy from Isaiah:

He will destroy in this mountain,
The covering that is cast over all people,
And the veil that is spread over all nations.
He will swallow up death in victory.

(*Isaiah* 25:7–8)

CHAPTER EIGHT

JESUS was arrested by the Jewish council through its usual police force, a group of men assigned to maintain order and make arrests. The Gospel of John calls them "a band of men and officers from the chief priests and Pharisees," (*John* 18:3) and this is probably a reasonable description. Matthew calls it "a great multitude with swords and staves, from the chief priests and elders," (*Matthew* 26:47) and Mark uses the same phrasing. There is no reason, however, why the council should have sent out a "multitude" or have attracted one, since they had planned to make the arrest as secretly as possible.

No Roman soldiers can have been present, for the arrest was not conducted under Roman orders and Jesus was not taken to the military barracks. He was taken instead to "the high priest's house." (*Luke* 22:54) Peter followed at a distance, and as he waited outside he was recognized as a Galilean by his speech and accused of being a follower of Jesus. He denied it three times in the course of the night, and "while he yet spake, the cock crew." (*Luke* 22:60)

Meanwhile, Jesus was being questioned by Annas, who

was the father-in-law of the high priest. Annas had once
held that office himself, so that he kept the honor as a
courtesy title and had a seat in the council. Five of his
sons later became high priests, and there are some Jewish
verses of the period which complain of the family influence exerted by such men.

> They are the high priests,
>   And their sons the treasurers;
> Their sons-in-law are Temple officers,
>   And their servants beat the people with their staves.

Annas obviously had a great deal of influence, and it
was natural that he should be the first to question Jesus.
He asked him about his teachings, and Jesus pointed out
that he had never taught secretly. "I spake openly to the
world; I ever taught in the synagogue, and in the temple,
where all Jews come together; and in secret have I said
nothing. Why asketh thou me? Ask them which heard
me, what I have said unto them." (*John* 18:20–21) One
of the officers standing by struck him for insubordina-
tion, and Jesus said, "If I have spoken evil, bear witness
of the evil; but if well, why smitest thou me?" (*John*
18:23) Annas was not in the habit of listening to un-
answerable questions, and he sent Jesus to his son-in-law,
Caiaphas.

Caiaphas, as high priest, was head of the council, and
he called a meeting that night. Not many of the members
had to be present, since twenty-three constituted a
quorum. Matthew and Mark say that they heard wit-

nesses, and there was probably an outward effort to conduct the meeting fairly. But the leaders of the council had already made up their minds that Jesus must be executed, and the chief reason for the meeting was probably to gather some kind of evidence that the Roman governor would accept. The council itself had no authority to execute Jesus. "It is not lawful for us to put any man to death." (*John* 18:31)

The meeting that night was probably less of a trial than an examination. The council members had to draw up a bill of particulars strong enough to convince Pilate that Jesus must be executed, and the three-part accusation recorded in the Gospel of Luke probably preserves the gist of it. "We found this fellow perverting the nation, and forbidding to give tribute to Caesar, and saying that he himself is Christ a king." (*Luke* 23:2) To this they added the further warning, "He stirreth up the people." (*Luke* 23:5)

Pontius Pilate knew by personal experience how easy it was to stir up the people in the crowded, emotional city of Jerusalem. When he first took office, he had permitted his soldiers to carry their military standards into the city. The Jews rioted, because medallions of the emperor were attached to the standards and they were therefore blasphemous. Pilate gave in on that occasion, and since then he had evidently been careful to inform himself on Jewish religious laws. When Jesus was brought to him in the judgment hall, Pilate met the members of the Jewish council outside. "They themselves went not into the judgment hall, lest they should be defiled; but that they might eat the passover." (*John* 18:28)

Pilate returned to the judgment hall to question Jesus and asked him the one thing that mattered from the Roman point of view: "Art thou the king of the Jews?" (*John* 18:33) If Jesus had said that he was, this would have been a clear case of treason against the emperor, and the death sentence would have been mandatory. Instead, Jesus asked a question of his own. "Sayest thou this thing of thyself, or did others tell it thee of me?" (*John* 18:34) Pilate retorted, "Am I a Jew? Thine own nation and the chief priests have delivered thee unto me. What hast thou done?" (*John* 18:35)

Jesus replied, as usual, by going straight to the point. "My kingdom is not of this world; if my kingdom were of this world, then would my servants fight, that I should not be delivered to the Jews." (*John* 18:36) This assured Pilate that Jesus was not a political agitator, but something about the prisoner made him want to go on with the questioning. He asked him of what his kingdom consisted, and Jesus gave the extraordinary answer that summarized the whole of his ministry. "To this end was I born, and for this cause came I into the world, that I should bear witness unto the truth." (*John* 18:37)

It is clear that Pilate was anxious not to get involved in any internal Jewish disputes over religion and equally clear that he was being hard pressed by the powerful Jewish council. When he discovered that Jesus was from Galilee he thought he saw an avenue of escape, for this put the prisoner technically under the jurisdiction of King Herod. Herod was in Jerusalem for the Passover, and Pilate sent Jesus to him.

It is reported in the Gospel of Luke that "when Herod saw Jesus, he was exceeding glad; for he was desirous to see him of a long season, because he had heard many things of him; and he hoped to have seen some miracle done by him." (*Luke* 23:8) King Herod had every reason to be aware of Jesus; the wife of one of his treasury officials, a woman named Joanna, had become a follower of Jesus, and later on a member of his court was active in the early Christian church.

When Herod first heard that Jesus was teaching in Galilee, he was afraid that John the Baptist, whom he had murdered, had somehow returned. At one time he had tried to see Jesus, and then, equally unsuccessfully, he had tried to kill him. Jesus had sent a message to the man he called "that fox" (*Luke* 13:32) when they were both in Galilee, but now that they were face to face in Judea he "answered him nothing." (*Luke* 23:9) The ruler of Galilee was in good standing with the emperor Tiberius, but he had nothing to say that Jesus considered worth answering.

Herod sent Jesus back to Pilate, and Pilate reported to the council that he had "found no fault in this man, touching those things whereof ye accuse him. No, nor did Herod, for he sent him back to us. Behold, nothing deserving death has been done by him." (*Luke* 23:15)

The Jewish council could not permit itself to accept

defeat. By every rule of what it called safety it dared not. There still remained one weapon in its hands, but this was a weapon that Pilate feared more than any other. It was the threat of riots in Jerusalem. If the Roman emperor heard that the governor of Judea was incapable of maintaining order, he would remove him from office.

Pilate was reluctant to sacrifice an innocent man, but he preferred that to sacrificing himself. In his eyes, the matter was probably one of those unpleasant cases in which an unfair decision is forced upon a public official for reasons of expediency. He made one final attempt to save Jesus, and when that was unsuccessful he ordered the execution.

Death by crucifixion was a routine punishment, and on one occasion alone a Roman official had crucified two thousand Jews outside the gates of Jerusalem. It was never used against a Roman, since that method of execution was considered a degradation, but it was a common sentence for rebels, slaves, and the lower type of criminal. Jesus underwent the usual punishment for all convicted malefactors of this type—the scourging, the carrying of the cross and the actual crucifixion. There were "two thieves crucified with him, one on the right hand, and another on the left," (*Matthew* 27:38) and the sentence was carried out by Roman soldiers.

The official charge against Jesus was that he had claimed to be the king of the Jews, and this title was written out on the cross. Pilate knew that the indictment was unjust, and so did the council. But they were all caught up in the responsibilities of government, doing what they believed to be best, and it cannot be held against a blind man that he should be an enemy of the light. Jesus himself looked on his murderers and felt nothing but compassion. "Father, forgive them; for they know not what they do." (*Luke* 23:34)

Of all that Jesus had to endure, perhaps the worst was the cry of the crowd that God had failed him. "He saved others; himself he cannot save . . . He trusted in God; let Him deliver him now." (*Matthew* 27:42–43)

As he hung nailed to the cross and the soldiers cast lots for his garments, Jesus remembered a psalm that in his case had become a prophecy.

> All they that see me laugh me to scorn . . . saying,
> He trusted on the Lord that He would deliver him. . . .
> The assembly of the wicked have enclosed me;
> They pierced my hands and my feet. . . .
> They part my garments among them,
> And cast lots upon my vesture.
>
> (*Psalms* 22:7, 8, 16, 18)

Jesus spoke the first line of the psalm aloud:

> My God, my God, why hast Thou forsaken me?
>
> (*Psalms* 22:1)

But he would not have forgotten that it continues through a catalogue of mounting terrors, and that it does not end until there is final victory.

> For the kingdom is the Lord's.
>
> (*Psalms* 22:28)

The watching crowd heard Jesus speak the first line aloud, (*Matthew* 27:46) and they misunderstood what he was saying. They thought he was calling on the prophet Elijah and they said to each other, "Let us see whether Elijah will come to save him." (*Matthew* 27:49) Then Jesus spoke again in the language of Scripture: "Father, into Thy hands I commend my spirit." (*Luke* 23:46) This again is a quotation from the Book of Psalms and an expression of perfect faith.

> Thou art my strength.
> Into Thine hand I commit my spirit.
> Thou hast redeemed me, O Lord God of truth.
> (*Psalms* 31:4–5)

Then he said, "It is finished," (*John* 19:30) and died.

It was three o'clock in the afternoon, six hours after the crucifixion had begun. Normally the men would have remained hanging on the crosses for another day at least, but the Sabbath began at sundown and this year the Sabbath coincided with the beginning of the Passover. In order that "the bodies should not remain upon the cross on the sabbath day (for that sabbath day was an high day)" (*John* 19:31) the Jewish authorities asked Pilate to finish the execution. It was possible for the victims of a crucifixion to stay alive for a day or more by supporting the weight of the body in part against the footrest to keep the blood from draining from the heart, and the Jews asked Pilate "that their legs might be broken" (*John* 19:31) so that they would die at once. The well-trained

Roman soldiers did their work thoroughly. When they reached Jesus he was already dead, but one of the soldiers drove a spear into his side to make sure.

One of the members of the Jewish council made a further request of Pilate, and it was an heroic one under the circumstances. He asked permission to give Jesus burial. Joseph of Arimathea had not been able to protect him from either the Jews or the Romans, but at least he had enough power to protect his body. Together with Nicodemus, his fellow member on the council, he took "the body of Jesus, and wound it in linen clothes with the spices, as the manner of the Jews is to bury." (*John* 19:40) Since it was almost sundown, they could not take the body far; they laid it in a tomb in a garden in the place where he had been crucified.

For the next twenty-four hours, all normal activity was forbidden among the Jews. The tomb was not visited until the day after the Sabbath, which was "the first day of the week" (*John* 20:1) or Sunday by the Christian calendar. Each of the gospels tells the story a little differently, but the details are handled most clearly and vividly in the Gospel of John.

According to the Fourth Gospel, a follower of Jesus whose name was Mary of Magdala came to the tomb so early that it was still dark. She found the stone in front of it rolled away, and she ran to tell two of the disciples, Peter and John. They entered the tomb and found it empty, the linen wrappings that Joseph and Nicodemus had used lying on the ground, "and the napkin, that was about his head, not lying with the linen clothes, but wrapped together in a place by itself." (*John* 20:7) Then the two disciples went away, and Mary stood weeping by the tomb.

> She turned herself back, and saw Jesus standing, and knew not that it was Jesus. Jesus saith unto her, "Woman, why weepest thou? Whom seekest thou?" She, supposing him to be the gardener, saith unto him, "Sir, if thou have borne him hence, tell me where thou hast laid him, and I will take him away." Jesus saith unto her, "Mary." She turned herself, and saith unto him, "Rabboni," which is to say, Master. Jesus saith unto her, "Touch me not; for I am not yet ascended to my Father: but go to my brethren, and say unto them, I ascend unto my Father, and your Father; and to my God, and your God.
> (*John* 20:14–17)

Three days earlier, in an upstairs room in Jerusalem, Jesus had told his disciples that he would no longer call them servants, but friends. (*John* 15:15) Now that he was prepared to go among them for the last time, having given final proof of what he meant by the fatherhood of God, he called them his brothers.

CHAPTER NINE

THERE have been many attempts to explain away the resurrection of Jesus, but none of them accounts for what happened in Jerusalem in the months that followed this particular feast of the Passover. A group of obscure Galileans were the followers of a local prophet who became discredited and died a criminal's death. A short time after his burial they were transformed, so driven by a single dominant conviction that nothing could stop them. This conviction was that Jesus must have been the Messiah, for he had risen from the dead.

It is true that this was not the manifestation of the Messiah that had been promised. "We have heard out of the law that Christ abideth for ever." (*John* 12:34) The message that the disciples carried all through Jerusalem did not have the support of any tradition behind it. It had one support only: the fact they knew it had happened.

Some of the disciples found it difficult to believe in the resurrection. (*Luke* 24:41) As one of them said, "Except I shall see in his hands the print of the nails, and put my finger into the print of the nails, and thrust my hand into his side, I will not believe." (*John* 20:25) But once they had seen with their own eyes and felt with their own hands, nothing could shake them.

In the beginning, the people who had seen Jesus alive after the crucifixion had no intention of forming a church of their own. All that Peter wanted the people of Jerusalem to know was that Jesus of Nazareth had not been destroyed by the crucifixion. He was "a man approved of God . . . whom God hath raised up, having loosed the pains of death; because it was not possible that he should be held by it." (*Acts* 2:22, 24) "This Jesus hath God raised up, whereof we all are witnesses." (*Acts* 2:32)

Peter made a large number of converts in Jerusalem, and the council was finally obliged to arrest him. This was the same Peter who had once sat in terror in the courtyard of the high priest and denied that he had anything to do with Jesus, but now he was quite unaffected by what the high priest could do to him. He was acting under a better authority. "The God of our fathers raised up Jesus . . . and we are his witnesses." (*Acts* 5:30, 32) One of the council members was a very wise Pharisee named Gamaliel, and he advised his fellow members to let Peter and the other apostles go free. "Let them alone: for if this counsel or this work be of men, it will come to nought: but if it be of God, ye cannot overthrow it; lest haply ye be found even to fight God." (*Acts* 5:38–39)

There was another member of this same sect, "a Pharisee and the son of Pharisees" (*Acts* 23:6) named Saul. In time he became a follower of Jesus and took the new

name of Paul. Like him, everyone in the new movement
was a Jew. It was to the Jews that Jesus had brought his
message of salvation, and when his followers went to
spread the gospel abroad they brought "the word to none
but unto the Jews only." (*Acts* 11:19) If any Gentile wished
to join the movement he had to submit to circumcision;
and in a city like Antioch, where "the disciples were
called Christians first," (*Acts* 11:26) they would still have
been looked upon as a Jewish sect.

Eventually, as the missionary work increased, some of
the leaders of the movement began to question the as-
sumption that anyone who wished to be a Christian must
first become a Jew, and a meeting was finally called in
Jerusalem to discuss the matter. One side maintained that
no convert to Christianity could be accepted unless he
entered through the door of Judaism. "It was needful to
circumcise them, and to command them to keep the law
of Moses." (*Acts* 15:5) It was the contrary view that
triumphed, and from that time on it was possible to be
a Christian without first becoming a Jew.

This decision was a special victory for Paul, the one-
time Pharisee. Paul had become convinced that the
sense of separateness which had sustained the Jewish
nation for so long was no longer necessary in the new
kind of freedom that Jesus brought. "There is neither
Jew nor Greek, there is neither bond nor free, there is
neither male nor female; for ye are all one in Christ Jesus.
And if ye be Christ's, then are ye Abraham's seed, and
heirs according to the promise." (*Galatians* 3:28–29)

The promise had been to the sons of Abraham; and yet the great prophets of Israel had never believed that it would continue to be confined to a single race.

> It is too light a thing that thou shouldest be My servant
> To raise up the tribes of Jacob,
> And to restore the preserved of Israel.
> I will also give thee for a light to the Gentiles,
> That My salvation may reach to the end of the earth.
>
> *(Isaiah* 49:6)

The discovery that Jesus brought into the world could never have been a matter of race nor confined to one people alone. Nevertheless, it was a single race that brought him forth, and it was the devotion of a single nation to God that made his ministry possible. As Jesus himself said, "Salvation is of the Jews." (*John* 4:22)

Never before and never again in the history of the world did a nation deserve the title of honor that is incorporated in the name Israel, the striver with God. The prophets were right when they promised a Day of the Lord, for it was inevitable, out of such a warfare, that victory should finally come.